Behind the Smiles

Tales from life in Thailand

Jane Fucella

Onwards and Upwards Publishers

3 Radfords Turf, Cranbrook, Exeter,
EX5 7DX, United Kingdom.
www.onwardsandupwards.org

This first edition published in the United Kingdom by Onwards and Upwards Publishers (2016).

ISBN:	978-1-911086-59-8
Typeface:	Sabon LT
Illustrations:	Mike Fucella
Author photograph:	Ivy Road Photography
Graphic design:	LM Graphic Design

Printed in the United Kingdom.

Scripture quotations are taken from the New Century Version®. Copyright © 2005 by Thomas Nelson. Used by permission. All rights reserved.

The story of Dee on page 96 was included by kind permission of William Carey Library. It was first published in *Suffering Christian Reflection on Buddhist Dukka* as part of the SEANET series.

The story of Sandy on page 123 was included by kind permission of SPCK. It was first published in *Church Communities confronting HIV and AIDS;* ISG 44.

Disclaimer: The events in this book are written from the perspective of the author and how she remembers them. She has sought to present a factual account, although some names have been changed to protect the identities of the people mentioned.

About the Author

Jane was born in Kenya and grew up in Oxfordshire. She trained as a general and then paediatric nurse and in 1983 visited Thailand for the first time. She and her husband Mike subsequently worked in Thailand together for twenty-two years initially sent by the Church of Scotland and latterly by Interserve Scotland. She has two daughters, Rachel and Aylie. Jane and Mike now live in Biggar, Scotland where Mike is minister of their local Church of Scotland church. Jane remains very involved in cross-cultural mission, and serves on the international council of Interserve.

Contact Details

ADDRESS

Jane Fucella
c/o Onwards and Upwards Publishers
3 Radfords Turf
Exeter
EX5 7DX

EMAIL

authorbehindthesmiles@gmail.com

FACEBOOK

www.facebook.com/behindthesmiles

 Scan the barcode to go straight to the book's Facebook page.

TWITTER

#behindthesmiles

Endorsements

Living and working for the Lord Jesus in a cross-cultural setting is a rich, faith-growing experience, but one where we are constantly ambushed by the unexpected or misunderstood. Jane Fucella's story of her family's years in Thailand shows how God delights to transform our mistakes and shortcomings, and makes the gospel shine through. This book shows how Christian faith lived out in love in a distant culture brings new life, hope and grace where it is so badly needed. Read; enjoy; pray for Thailand!

Rose Dowsett
Speaker and Author
Former International Chairman of Interserve

Jane Fucella has written a moving, honest, perceptive and humorous account of over twenty years serving the church in Thailand with her husband and two daughters. In their range of roles – nursing, preaching, land development, child protection, teaching, community building, church leadership training, mentoring – Jane narrates tales of heart-breaking sadness and injustice, 'man's inhumanity to man'; but also experiences of inspiration and healing, witnessing to the hand and grace of God at work. As the title hints, sometimes appearances belie the reality, and Jane explores some of the difficulties behind cross-cultural and integral mission, and what it means to 'trust and obey' completely as a follower of Jesus. What comes through is not only Jane's desire to 'bring good news to the poor, and to bind up the broken-hearted, and set people free', but her unswerving love for God, her deep compassion for people, and her delight in responding to the call of God.

Rev. David Lunan
Former Moderator, Church of Scotland

Jane has chosen to write, not a chronological account of their missionary years, but rather a collection of snapshot chapters, dealing with topics like: learning the languages (and dropping some linguistic clangers); pets and wildlife (getting used – and never getting used – to snakes, rats and multiple creepy-crawlies); understanding and respecting the culture, beliefs and religious traditions, incorporating them, if at all theologically possible, into Christian practice; medical emergencies, both family and friends/neighbours; squaring up to the challenge of Thai food – its cooking, storage and choice of ingredients; and the delights and dangers of various modes of transport.

Through it all shines Jane's passionate and tender care for everyone she meets and especially for those in her care, as she nursed and supported men, women, children and whole families through the early days of HIV and AIDS. Theirs was a holistic mission. They took Jesus' love, through practical care, to those in the most dire need, demonstrating acceptance, forgiveness and hope, and often creating an open door to take the gospel through and into the lives and souls of their Thai flock.

Buddhism is woven into the Thai psyche: 'To be Thai is to be Buddhist is to be Thai.' This fascinating account of life in Thailand – as missionaries, as neighbours and friends, as husband and wife, as parents, as farmers, as medical practitioners, as survivors – lifts the lid on what it means to practise and seek to spread the Christian faith in such a situation. It is a must-read for everyone considering Christian mission work in any land; but it will also be a must-read for all of us who support and pray for our missionaries.

Fran Brady
Scottish Author
Editor of WordWise,
    the magazine of the Scottish Fellowship of Christian Writers.

This is a missionary story the like of which we have never seen before! Beautifully written, delightfully illustrated, it is packed with fascinating detail from lives motivated by the compassion of Jesus in the struggle to live in different cultures and to serve other people. It is funny – at times hilarious – but very honest in relating a significant and highly instructive experience of cross-cultural mission. Jane's wonderful account will assist a new generation preparing to 'live on terms set by others', but it should [also] be read by people in Western churches trying to adjust to the presence of Asian immigrants within their communities and congregations.

Dr David Smith
Honorary Lecturer in Aberdeen University

Contents

Foreword by Paul Bendor-Samuel

There's a lot of confusion in mission today.

Like many things at this moment in history, old certainties have given way to doubts in the face of rapid change. For some in the post-Christian West, the idea of sending Christians in mission is unthinkable: they don't need us, it's just Christian colonialism, and anyway, the needs are too great here. For others, it is business as usual; the call to send missionaries is simply part of the mandate of the church. They continue with the same approach and slogans, seemingly ignorant of the birth and growth of the church in even the most difficult and hostile environments around the world.

For still others, the confusion lies with the very nature of mission and the gospel. There has been a welcome growth in understanding that mission is not primarily what the church does but is God's. We participate in God's mission because He calls us to join Him in what He is doing. Yet the past fifty years has witnessed strident battles between those who reduce mission to simply verbal proclamation of the gospel and those who claim a more holistic understanding, while in practice almost exclusively focusing on acts of compassion, education or business.

Behind the Smiles shines the spotlight on mission today, cutting through the fog of confusion. Jane Fucella writes in a simple, engaging style that is both authentic and reflective. Through the stories of fun and tragedy, breakthroughs and setbacks, glorious church and genuine failure, Jane shows us what following Jesus in cross-cultural mission is all about.

What emerges through the narrative is that yes, God is building His church and yes, there is a tremendous role alongside this church for ordinary brothers and sisters who are prepared to draw alongside and share the load together. What emerges is that yes, the truth of the gospel proclaimed changes lives and that this can never be separated from practically sharing in the pain and brokenness of those we serve.

To try to prioritise one over the other is to completely miss the nature of salvation – they simply cannot and must not be separated.

Jane's stories illustrate another vital principle in mission today. God is at work and the primary work of the cross-cultural mission worker in most places is to enable the local church to better participate in this work. In Interserve we repeatedly ask our people the question, 'In what way will this ministry empower the local church to participate more fully in God's mission?' Over their twenty years in Thailand, Jane and Mike had the privilege of working at different levels with the church: local, regional and national. Not all are called to exercise such strategic influence. At the same time, Jane and Mike, with their children Rachel and Aylie, model at different stages of their journey a wide range of roles alongside the church that all can learn from. It always starts with friendship and includes prayer, spiritual warfare, acts of service, co-pioneering, teaching, mentoring, equipping leaders and growing locally appropriate discipleship and theology. As you read the stories, try to identify the rich range of roles being played out in order that the church might better participate in God's mission.

My wife and I have known Jane and Mike for thirty years. I am thrilled to see this book in print because what you read here is for real. I cannot think of anyone I know who better models mission today. Enjoy, be inspired and be available!

Paul Bendor-Samuel
Executive Director of the Oxford Centre for Mission Studies and former International Director of Interserve

PREFACE

Tales from Thailand

'Gillie, grab the red metal toolbox and bring it to me outside the front of the house as fast as you can.' I was already out of the church door as I screamed these rather strange instructions to my sister who was following me in a state of bemused confusion.

We had been taking part in a women's conference in the church where Mike and I served in Sivilai, a village in north-east Thailand. Just being there was a culture shock for my visiting sister, as she adjusted to the oppressive humidity and heat, sat on the floor listening to Bible teaching in a language she had never heard before, or was dragged to her feet to dance to very loud traditional local worship music.

The previous day had involved an uncomfortable, dusty, five-hour drive to Sivilai from the city, sharing the back of the pick-up truck with a very large, very much alive pig, who was destined to provide the meals for the conference. The early hours of the morning brought with them the squeals of said pig as he was despatched and the first meal prepared, to the tune of ear-splittingly loud music blasting out of the six-foot-high loud speakers. And then suddenly I was screaming at her above the noise of the amplified music.

I had seen a young man called Wud being driven dangerously fast into the church compound in a three-wheel motorised *samlor*[1] and knew immediately that there was something wrong. Somehow Gillie found the box and arrived at the front door as I appeared with a very

---

[1] rickshaw

distressed Wud, who had blood pouring from his hands. Once again I was yelling instructions at her: 'Open it up and get me all the sanitary towels you can find and a couple of plastic bags.' She looked even more bemused but did as she was told and watched me put the bags on my hands, rip the towels out of their packaging and whack them onto Wud's hands. These were not the expected contents of a toolbox. Using individually wrapped sanitary towels to mop up blood and apply pressure to a wound was one of many useful things I had learnt in the few years we had been in Sivilai. The unavailability of sterile gloves, combined with the increasing incidence of HIV in north-east Thailand at that time, meant that any first aid kit (mine was in a large metal concertina-type toolbox) always contained plastic bags which could be used as makeshift gloves in emergencies. As the bleeding slowed down, and I dealt as well as I could with his wounds, we went inside.

Once he had stopped shaking, Wud explained that he had smashed his hands through a glass pane in a fit of uncontrollable rage. He was a disturbed kid who struggled with mental illness, following his two years of national service in the military, and eventually died of an AIDS-related illness at the age of twenty-five. He was one of many whom we loved, who passed through our doors and impacted our lives, during our adventure of ministry in Thailand.

This book is a compilation of stories of people like Wud and events in our lives that make up our journey of twenty-five years in Thailand. Chapter 1 tells how we got to Thailand in the first place. Thereafter the stories are arranged thematically rather than chronologically. If this seems at times confusing, then take a look at the Reference section on page 13, which will give you an idea of the chronology of events and places where we lived, as well as showing their locations on a map.

REFERENCE

Where and When: A Reader's Guide

Bangkok, March 1990 - March 1991

Our first year in Bangkok was devoted to language study. It was only many years later we appreciated what a privilege it was to have so long to spend learning language with no other responsibilities. A friend kindly gave us a house rent-free. It had previously been a factory and the ground floor was fairly derelict, but we had two large rooms and a bathroom, so plenty of space for us and for guests. All we had to pay was the ten pounds a month land rent to the King, as the house was built on his land! This is apparently quite common in Bangkok but seemed special to us. The house backed onto a secondary school and was walking distance to the commercial centre with all the big shopping complexes, and an easy bus ride to language school.

Udon Thani, March - August 1991

When we had first approached the Church of Christ in Thailand (CCT) leadership about serving in Thailand we asked if we could work amongst the poorest of the poor. We had both done a lot of reading about God's heart for the poor, simple lifestyle and incarnational-type mission as well as encouraging the church to be relevant to the local context (contextualisation). We wanted to live with people at a grass-roots level in order to understand the culture well enough to present a gospel that was relevant to them at a heart level. It was therefore suggested that we go to the north-east of Thailand, also known as Isaan

13

and considered to be the poorest part of the country. We visited a couple of times during our language year and got to know the leaders of the presbytery in Udon Thani. I think from the beginning they thought we were odd, but they were not going to turn down free workers.

On 27th March, 1991, exactly one year after our arrival in Bangkok, we took a six-wheel truck piled high with our belongings and our dog Danny and drove the three hundred and fifty miles to our new home in Udon. We lived at the presbytery centre, just outside the city. It had once been a Bible school and fish farm but by 1991 was offices and a centre for presbytery-wide annual revival meetings. A few church families lived at the centre and we were given a small wooden house on stilts to make our home. It had a bathroom downstairs, with walls that did not meet the roof, and a bedroom and office upstairs. We learnt how to shower by throwing cold water over ourselves, how to do laundry in buckets under the house, how to cook outside on a charcoal stove (just learning how to light it was a lesson in itself), how to put up and then sleep under a mosquito net and how to deal with a python in the bathroom.

We visited a different church every Sunday, spread over an area the size of Wales. I am sure they were sussing us out just as much as we were trying to suss them out in our search for the place to settle. Despite a year at language school our Thai was very basic. Locals were very patient with us – I think we thought we were quite good! – as they sat through our sermons. I am sure we prayed and asked God for guidance but what I remember is visiting Sivilai and knowing, 'This is it.' Apart from anything else it was the most remote place and farthest from the presbytery leaders, who, we could already sense, didn't always agree with our ideas – in retrospect, very arrogant ideas – of a simple lifestyle, incarnational ministry and contextualisation!

Sivilai, August 1991 - December 1998

Sivilai was officially a *'tambon'* – the designation given to a community with a population somewhere between being a village and a district town.[2] There was a vibrant market, one paved road running

---

[2] During our time there it was elevated to district town status.

through the town, and electricity but no mains water, sewage or phone lines. Our nearest phone was half an hour's drive away on the motorbike. No supermarkets, Internet, sit down loos or other mod cons!

As far as we knew, the only other expats were in Nong Khai, just over a hundred miles away, and we met no one who spoke English. Sivilai Fellowship Church (*Kristjak Sivilai Samaki* in Thai) had about twenty regular members, mainly second-generation Christians who had moved from cities farther south in Isaan. One large extended family was dominant and controlled much of what happened in the church. For our first six months we lived with Bee and Ken, a couple from that family, and their four teenage sons. They generously gave us the only divided off room in the house – and even then the walls stopped about a foot from the ceiling.

We stayed in Sivilai until December 1998. It was a rollercoaster seven years, spiritually and emotionally. We saw God work in amazing ways and were privileged to be involved in many people's lives and in different areas of ministry as we led the church. Our daughter Rachel was born in 1994, and was embraced by the church and town community as we had been. She was nearly five when we left. As the church grew from twenty members to a hundred and fifty, there were, like everywhere, powerful people who did not want change. Some of the presbytery leaders also felt unhappy with the direction the church moved in – lay leadership, local music, etc. – and so on several occasions, usually when we were in the UK on home assignment, there were attempts made by some people to get rid of us. It was very painful and I can remember crying myself to sleep often. But we were sure it was where we were meant to be and we were seeing real fruit.

Eventually, it seemed right to look for a Thai pastor to take over from us and in May 1998 Py and Nip arrived. We spent the next seven months working with them, before we left Sivilai for good and went on study leave in Scotland in January 1999.

Scotland, January 1999 - October 2000

We were in Scotland for nearly two years. During this time our daughter Aylie was born, and Mike did a master's degree in Theology,

Culture and Development at New College in Edinburgh. We also did the organisation, planning and running of an international missions conference for all the Church of Scotland overseas partner churches, in St. Andrews. At three months old Aylie was the star of the show.

While we were in the UK, we had no idea which part of Thailand we would return to. We assumed it would be Isaan, particularly with our knowledge of the local language and culture. However, it became clear that the presbytery leaders wanted us back to live in Udon city and do what we felt was 'hit and run' ministry to the villages. This was not something we had a vision for at all, which left us in a dilemma about the future.

Not long before we were due to return to Thailand, an invitation came out of the blue for us to serve a presbytery in the west of the country, working with the Karen church. We had no idea about the situation there, but it felt right, so we and the Church of Scotland said, 'Yes, please!' When we returned to Thailand in October 2000, Rachel was six-and-a-half and had experienced just over a year in a Scottish primary school. Aylie was almost eighteen months old.

Sangklaburi, October 2000 - March 2005

Sangklaburi lies close to the Thai-Burmese border. It is on the far edges of Kanchanaburi province, about four hours' drive north-west of Kanchanaburi city, famous for the Bridge over the River Kwai and the Second World War death railway. Sangklaburi, or 'New Town' as it is known locally, is a small town built on the edge of a huge man-made lake surrounded by jungle. There has been a Christian presence in the area since the late 1950s when Karen families moved from Chiang Rai as missionaries to reach out to the Karen coming over the border from Burma. At about the same time, missionaries from America started a mission station with a church, school and hospital on the banks of the River Kwai. From 1983 to 1985 the government, with help from a team of Australian engineers, constructed a dam across the river. A massive lake was formed which filled with water within just a few days of the dam's completion. The new Sangklaburi was built on the lakeshore and included government schools and a hospital. Saha mission school and Kwai River Christian Hospital were therefore relocated to a predominantly Karen relocation community about twelve miles away, near to the border.

Having worked entirely at a local church level in Sivilai, Mike was asked to work at a presbytery level, living in a rural church community on the edge of Sangklaburi town, but helping develop lay leaders across the whole presbytery[3]. Although most presbyteries in the CCT are purely geographical, some are also specific to an ethnic group. This presbytery is almost entirely Karen and it was with this Karen church that Mike ministered. He worked with a team of Karen church leaders, who became his closest friends. Although Mike's main role was visiting and training of church leaders we were able to get involved in many areas of church and community life. I think our few years in Sangklaburi were our happiest in Thailand.

However, by 2005 it was clearly time to move again. I had, with help from volunteer teachers, home-schooled the girls but by the time Rachel was eleven we felt she needed to be in an international school. Aylie too, by then aged six, needed English-speaking peers to relate to. She spoke good Burmese, Karen and Thai but had no children, except her sister, to really talk with in English. At the same time the Church of Scotland pulled out of placing partners in Thailand, making us redundant, so we had to look for a new mission agency.

Bangkok, August 2005 - June 2012

In March 2005 we returned to Scotland and applied to Interserve. We were accepted, visited our forty partner churches, raised the necessary financial support and were back in Thailand for the beginning of the children's school year in Bangkok in early August. Having worked at a local level in Sivilai and a presbytery level in Sangklaburi, Mike was invited to work at a national level at the CCT headquarters and also an international level with the member countries of the Mekong Ecumenical Partnership Program[4]. In addition, he was asked by the CCT to teach Christian Ethics at the Bangkok Institute of Theology, their seminary in the capital city.

---

[3] three hundred miles running south from Sangklaburi along the Thai-Burmese border

[4] MEPP – Thailand, Laos, Cambodia, Burma and Vietnam

I filled various roles in Bangkok. I returned to prison work, spending a day a week in the maximum security prison hospital working mainly with people who had AIDS. I took on a leadership role for Interserve in the region for five years and I did one-on-one mentoring with both Thai and ex-pat Christians. I also worked on the staff team at Christ Church International Anglican church for nearly two years.

We were in Bangkok for nearly seven years.

CHAPTER ONE

Our Journey to Thailand

Mike and I met in prison in Bangkok. Our kids love to tell people this and then just leave the conversation hanging in the air, allowing their audience to make their own, often inaccurate, assumptions! In fact, Mike and I got to know each other and started dating whilst *working* in a prison in Bangkok, but had met once before. In 1986 Mike applied for a volunteer job with Southeast Asian Outreach (SAO), a small mission agency working in the immigration detention centre in Bangkok, and I was on the interview panel. All I can really remember about that first encounter was that he had driven his motorbike from Scotland to London. Very cool!

In June 1987, about a year after first meeting Mike, I arrived to work at the immigration detention centre in central Bangkok for three months, between leaving my job at Guy's Hospital in London and going to study for two years at All Nations Christian College (ANCC) in Hertfordshire. Mike met me at Bangkok Airport and took me back to the mission house that we shared with a couple and their young son. A week later they went away and, as I sat at my desk typing my first aerogramme home, Mike went on bended knee and asked me out. Our first date was a smoothie stall on Soi Suan Phlu, the street where the detention centre was. Delicious fresh tropical fruit blended with ice, a splash of syrup and a sprinkle of salt, sucked up through thick straws whilst standing on the side of the road next to a bustling market, made it a first date to remember. The second date was a doughnut joint outside MBK, the biggest shopping centre I had ever seen. I was literally swept off my feet – I had never been on the back of a motorbike before! I particularly remember speeding down a newly constructed road. It was not yet open and we had the whole eight lanes to ourselves – wind in my hair and my arms around the man in my life!

The journeys that brought us each to Bangkok were very different. From as long as I could remember I had wanted to be a nurse. I made a commitment to Christ when I was eleven and from then on was determined to be used by Him in some way, but not necessarily as a missionary. In my final year of nurse training, several things happened that steered me in that direction, and particularly towards Thailand. I was clear in my mind that was where I was meant to be.

In October 1983, as soon as we finished our nursing training, my friend Nikki and I set off on the holiday of a lifetime. We had various connections in Thailand, mainly through Southeast Asian Outreach, whose work I had been supporting. Our month saw us visiting missionaries in Bangkok and in Ban Vinai refugee camp on the Laos border. We also had a wonderful few days at a mission guest house by the sea in Hua Hin, run by Robin and Geraldine – parents of a friend. They treated us like family and many of the stories they told and the people we met there were influential in my commitment to Thailand.

On one occasion Robin showed us a dead snake in the garden and carefully opened its mouth, explaining to us with passion how you differentiate between a poisonous and non-poisonous snake depending on whether it has teeth or fangs. I couldn't bring myself to tell him that there was no way I was ever going to waste time looking in a snake's mouth before bludgeoning it to death with the nearest long stick!

One person, whom we met purely by chance, had a profound impact on my life. Sadly, I cannot even remember her name. We were visiting one of the prisons when we came across an American woman sitting on a bench outside, enjoying a cool drink as she waited for a friend. It was hot, humid, smelly and noisy; a very uncomfortable place to sit. We were surprised to see her there, especially when we discovered that she was nearly ninety years old.

She told us her story. Soon after she and her husband had retired, he died. They had made many plans together for retirement and she was devastated at the loss of these precious years with him. However, after a while, she was convinced that God was saying these were her years to serve Him. For the next twenty years she spent six months of every year serving God through reaching out to others in some of the toughest places in Bangkok, like the prison where we met her. She said that over those twenty years she had been privileged to see God work in amazing ways.

There were two things she felt were key to serving God which she wanted to share with us and I believe she also wrote about in a book. The first was that we should be *available to God,* willing and open to be used by Him, however, wherever and whenever He chooses. No strings attached. No provisos. The second was that having made ourselves available we should be *obedient.* Obedient even if it means crossing the globe aged eighty plus, against all sensible advice. Obedient even if it means stepping out in faith as Abraham did, not knowing where God will lead. Obedient even if it means others get hurt by our obedience. I struggled with the idea of being obedient even if others get hurt by it. How could God allow that? Surely if our obedience means others are hurt, then we must have misunderstood...

Later, as Mike and I prepared to move to Thailand away from loved ones, knowing it would hurt them, I came across a piece of writing which helped me to see it a different way. Oswald Chambers writes in *My Utmost for His Highest* about trusting God, particularly regarding the consequences of our obedience:

> If we obey God it is going to cost other people more than it costs us and that is where the sting comes in. ... If we obey God it will mean that other people's plans are upset. ... If we obey God He will look after those who have been pressed into the consequences of our obedience. We have simply to obey and leave all the consequences to Him.[5]

---

[5] Taken from *My Utmost for His Highest*® by Oswald Chambers, edited by James Reimann, © 1992 by Oswald Chambers Publications Assn., Ltd., and used by permission of Discovery House, Grand Rapids MI 49501. All rights reserved.

Availability, obedience and trust – not easy, but when we manage to open ourselves up to God's leading, listen and obey Him and then trust Him to deal with the consequences, it is amazing where He leads us. That conversation outside a prison, with a woman whose name I no longer remember, was more important for my journey than either she or I realised at the time, and has remained with me ever since.

At the end of our brief sojourn in Thailand, when we were waiting at the airport for our flight back to the UK, I remember Nikki being sad about leaving after such a great month. All I felt was the certainty that Thailand was home and I would be back.

On my return to the UK I got more involved with promoting missions, traveling around the country speaking at churches and university Christian Unions about the work with refugees in Thailand. Eventually I applied to All Nations Christian College to do a two-year course in Missiology and Cross Cultural Studies. But, before starting in September 1987, I heard through SAO of a need for someone medical to help in the immigration detention centre where Mike was working. So I packed my bags and went to Bangkok for three months. That was the beginning of our journey together.

I cannot assume to tell the story of Mike's call in much detail. He is American and grew up as an army kid living in various countries around the world. When he eventually went to the USA to college he could not settle into American life and after two years he opted to transfer and moved to Aberdeen, in Scotland, to study for a Bachelor of Divinity specialising in Old Testament and Hebrew. At that time he believed he would have an academic future. However, Mike also helped out in a local church and found that academia didn't always help him to deal with the nitty-gritty of life, like bereavement or sickness. Consequently, Mike decided that he needed to serve in a very practical way for a few years before committing to the academic life. So he applied to SAO to work with illegal immigrants imprisoned in Bangkok, and it was there that we started our life together.

From then on I can honestly say it feels like we just followed the path that was in front of us. I can't tell stories of flashing lights or clear guidance about where we should go or what we should do. Things just seemed to happen. In 1988 I returned to Thailand to visit Mike for a month. I remember struggling to decide whether to say yes to his marriage proposal because I felt it was rather like a holiday romance and maybe in our real worlds it would be different. But then a friend said to me that I should not be thinking about whether I could live with Mike for the rest of my life, but rather, could I bear to live without him? I will never forget that conversation as Angela and I sat by the pool at the British Club – an oasis of calm in the chaos of Bangkok. It helped me make one of the most important decisions of my life – even though I didn't actually say yes until we were both back in the UK six months later.

We felt strongly that we wanted to live and serve in Thailand – not in a prison setting but with the Thai Church. So we went to see the leader[6] of the CCT, and asked him if they would like us to join them as mission partners and what we would need to do to be able to come back to work. He was enthusiastic and encouraging but said we should be sent by a partner church. So, when we got back to the UK we asked the Church of Scotland if we could go to Thailand. They did not, at that time, have an official partnership with the CCT but agreed, as long as we got through their selection process.

Later, in 1988, Mike moved to the UK and lived with my parents in Oxfordshire working on a fish farm and in a book warehouse as well as converting a five-hundred-year-old grain store in my parents' garden into a house for us. It was an excellent way for him to get to know his future in-laws, and vice versa. I think by the time our wedding day came they knew him a lot better than I did! I finished at All Nations and in July 1989 we were married. We went for interviews with the Church of Scotland Board of Mission while on our honeymoon, and in January 1990 moved to Edinburgh to get to know the Church of Scotland and meet our thirty partner churches. We eventually flew to Bangkok on 26th March, 1990, sent by the Church of Scotland to work under the CCT. Our adventure together in Thailand had begun a new chapter which lasted twenty-two years.

---

[6] Dr Boonrat Boayen, General Secretary at the time

CHAPTER TWO

Communication Skills in a New Culture

Thai is a tonal language with five different tones and seventy-six letters in the alphabet. The script is completely different from Western script, as is the grammar. Anyone wanting to communicate with people on a heart level – or, in fact, about anything outside of Bangkok – needs to learn Thai. A tonal language lends itself to some confusing and funny mistakes. For example, the word for 'near' is *'gly'* and the word for 'far' is *'gly'*, but with a different tone. A Thai person would not even consider the words to be similar because the tones matter so much. The words for 'silk', 'no', 'new' and 'fire' are the same but with different tones, as are the words for 'dog', 'horse' and 'come'!

We studied at Union Language School (ULS) for four intense hours every morning for most of our first year. I regularly got off the bus rather bedraggled, leaving behind a puddle on the floor where I had been standing, from the sweat running down my back and legs! And yet my fellow Thai passengers looked cool and immaculate. After school I think we were meant to do homework but I do not remember much of that. We got to know the kids in the local high school and ran some hilarious English lessons and went on trips with them.

We also got involved in running the youth group for the International Church of Bangkok (ICB) and I am sure we spent far more time with English speakers than we should have. However, our Thai did progress, much to my surprise. I had always struggled with school French and so assumed I was no good at languages. I think my need to talk a lot helped me! *'Pit ben khru'* – 'mistakes are your

25

teachers' – was drummed into us from early on, which meant we had to be willing to take risks and speak in order to improve. For someone who struggles to keep quiet this was not difficult and I made a lot of mistakes! The lessons were intense; no English allowed at all in the classroom from the first day. The headmistress had microphones in all the classrooms and rumour had it that teachers' pay was docked if she overheard them speaking English. They lived in fear of her and so we muddled along, and probably learnt quicker than we would have done if we had cheated.

We ran some hilarious English lessons.

In Isaan most people spoke Lao. The language of Laos is quite close to Thai. There are six tones rather than the five in Thai and they are used differently. There is quite a large amount of vocabulary that is also different. Lao has a different feel to the language – a lilt to it that makes me think it is spoken to a different tune. It is also always spoken at breakneck speed – or so it seemed to us. We tried to learn it and I think did reasonably well when in the company of Isaan people. When we moved to Sangklaburi I forgot Lao quite quickly but when we eventually moved back to Bangkok we were surrounded by Isaan migrant workers in the community where we lived. I found, after a few minutes of sitting chatting, the feel and unique rhythm of the language would come back and I could understand quite well, even if everyone laughed at my efforts to speak it.

Sangklaburi district has an international population dominated by people who have fled from Burma since the end of World War Two. There are many different tribal groups, each with their own language and culture. The town itself is made up predominantly of Po Karen, who are mainly Buddhist. The village where the hospital and school are located is predominantly Skaw Karen, many of whom are Christian. There are large communities of Mon[7], Burmese, and even people who have come from Bangladesh and Laos through Burma to Thailand. The district has several temples, including a Mon temple known for a famous abbot, and a place of pilgrimage for Buddhists from all over Thailand and even farther afield. There is also a lively Muslim mosque as well as several churches. The small, ethnically Thai community consists mainly of civil servants sent to work in the hospital, schools and government offices. And, of course, as in almost every community in Asia, there are the Chinese business people. On any day several different languages can be heard in the large fresh market in the centre of town. On the whole all the different groups in Sangklaburi appear to live peacefully together.

Mike was working with the Karen church so he valiantly learnt some Karen language; both the tones and script are different from Thai. By the time we left he could lead communion in Karen but never became good enough to preach in Karen. My patients spoke all the languages represented in the town so I stuck to English or Thai. I could do that because Doe, whom I worked closely with, spoke Burmese, English, Thai, Skaw Karen and Mon and was a brilliant translator! Our Thai language skills definitely suffered whilst we were living in Sangklaburi, as most of the people we conversed with spoke worse Thai than we did!

---

[7] mainly Buddhist and, interestingly, linguistically very close to the Khmer people in Cambodia

Thais are known for asking questions that we in the West would consider to be very personal; things like, 'What do you weigh?' or, 'How much do you earn?' or, 'Why aren't you married?' Once I was asked, 'Why don't you have kids?' closely followed by, 'What contraception do you use?' These are not questions that need to be answered directly. It is like someone in the UK asking, 'How are you?' – never for a minute expecting or wanting a full, honest answer.

However, there is one direct question that would rarely be asked in polite British society, but it is essential to answer honestly in Thailand: 'How old are you?' Respect, related to age hierarchy, is very important. How you greet someone, how you address them and how you refer to them all depends on the relative ages of those speaking and being spoken to or about. In order to get it right, it is essential to know the age of the person you are talking to – or at least know if they are older or younger than you are.

Once age has been established then appropriate titles can be used. A child, or someone clearly younger than you, is addressed as *'Nong'* usually followed by their name, but not necessarily. It means 'younger brother or sister' or, when on its own, just 'child'. Someone older than you but in roughly the same generation should be addressed as *'P'* followed by their name – it means 'older brother or sister'. Someone of your parents' generation is addressed as 'aunty' or 'uncle'. The Thai words are different depending on whether they are actually older or younger than your parents; people were amazed that I didn't know exactly how old my parents were! Someone of your grandparents' age may be addressed as 'granny' or 'granddad' – but if you are talking about actual grandparents then there are different words for maternal and paternal grandmothers and grandfathers. Are you confused yet? Of course, all of these titles are fairly informal. It was how we addressed people when we lived in villages. We were quite surprised to find that even people who were quite close friends might not actually know each other's names, just using titles like 'aunty' to address each other. In the cities titles are more formal. You never refer to anyone just by their name but always with the prefix *'khun'* which is basically a generic Mr, Mrs or Miss. Unless of course they have another title such as *'khru'* (teacher), *'mor'* (doctor, but used for almost anyone working in a hospital) and within the church *'phubakrong'* (elder) or *'ajan'*. *'Ajan'* means 'reverend' but is also used for university professors or, it seems, missionaries – it was what we were both called from day one.

The word 'I' is not used very often. In language school we each learnt a formal translation for 'I', two different words depending on whether the speaker is male or female. However, once we were out in the world, we discovered that most people refer to themselves not as 'I' but using their own name. So instead of saying, 'I am going to the shops,' I would say, 'Jane is going to the shops.' It was something I never really got used to. The other thing that took me a long time to even work out, let alone get used to doing myself, was the use of the word *'noo'*. 'Noo' means 'mouse' – or so I thought. However, it is also used as a diminutive to refer to oneself when talking to an older person or showing respect to someone of higher status. So when talking with a church leader or someone older than me I would not say 'I' or even 'Jane', but rather, 'Noo thinks that...' Again it took a long time before we were getting it right – or, I *think* we were getting it right!

Surnames are a relatively new phenomenon in Thailand, and even today many of our Karen friends who have come from Burma, even within the last generation, do not have one. Even those who do rarely use them. People address each other by their title followed by their given name, e.g. *Khun Jane*. This applies to everyone, from the Prime Minister, to the company director, to the street cleaner. Westerners working in Thailand have taken on the practice and when our children went to an international school we were not surprised that the teachers were addressed as Mr or Ms followed by their first name, rather than their surname – something that would have been unheard of when I was a child or even now in the UK. Additionally, almost everyone in Thailand has two given names. There is a long formal name which means something e.g. *Phonsawaan,* meaning 'blessing from heaven', and then a nickname which is what they are most often known by. We have many friends whose full name I have never even been told. Nicknames are hilarious and for people in the West often seem offensive. Names like *Uan* (fatty), *Maa* (dog), *Chang* (elephant), *Noi* (small) are very common and quite acceptable. Rachel and Aylie were both given Thai nicknames which were used by all the Thai people we knew. Rachel's name is *Nong Yui* (pronounced 'You-ee'). It means 'chubby cheeks'! Aylie's is *Nong Geew* (pronounced 'Gay-o') which means 'crystal'. When we moved to Sivilai the moderator of the presbytery gave Mike and me names, but more formal ones with meaning that was apparently perfect for us. Mike was *Ajan Tongdee* – 'good gold', we think, with reference to his reddish hair – and I was *Ajan Jansri*, 'the glory of the moon', presumably because it was close to 'Jane'. People would laugh at our names as there is a famous love story about a couple called Tongdee and Jansri!

When we moved to Sangklaburi Mike's name proved to be something of a problem. He could not understand why every time he was introduced as the Rev. Tongdee his team would do it with massive grins and the whole place would erupt in laughter. Eventually, they explained that the Karen tend to drop final consonants making his name sound like Rev. *To-dee* – the Karen word for 'long eggs', a euphemism for long or droopy testicles. No wonder they laughed when Rev. Long Testicles was introduced at the beginning of a service. Reluctantly the team agreed to forfeit their regular introductory joke and give him a new Karen name – *Tra Tu-a* – which means, like his Thai name, 'Rev. Good Gold'!

Traditionally, Thais do not shake hands when they meet someone. They *'wai'*. The wai is a graceful action practised throughout Thailand. It plays a very important part in showing respect and is central to Thai etiquette. It consists of bringing one's hands together as if praying, usually with the tips of the fingers just under the nose and the arms tucked in neatly – no flapping elbows! In wai etiquette, age is once again important and tells you when to initiate the wai. It can be difficult to determine when you should wai or when someone should wai you. The younger person should usually initiate the wai. However, when to wai also depends on your relationship to the other person. A person of clearly higher social status will be wai-ed to regardless of age, in the same way as an older person. It all seems very complicated and for years no one explained it to us, so we just wai-ed left, right, and centre and hoped we were covering ourselves and not offending anyone.

When being wai-ed to, you would be considered impolite if you didn't return the wai except perhaps to a child where a nod will do. However, it is difficult to wai back when you are carrying a lot of bags or in the middle of doing something like eating. The wai is, above all else, a symbol of the fact that relationship is the most important thing in Thai culture. So if someone greets you, you physically have to put aside or put down what you are carrying or doing – items, satisfying one's own needs etc. – to return the wai in order to pursue good relationships. Only monks and royalty are never expected to return a wai.

The wai is a useful thing to master, especially in the early days of language learning. We discovered a wai not only means 'hallo' and 'goodbye', but also 'thank you', 'I am sorry' and almost any other greeting you can think of – so very useful when linguistically challenged!

The Karen do not wai unless greeting someone Thai. The Karen shake hands! This took some getting used to after ten years of wai-ing. However, the handshake is slightly different from a British or American handshake. They shake right hands whilst at the same time holding the right elbow with the left hand. Historically it was a way of clearly showing that there was no weapon in the left hand. Some of the market stallholders still do the same thing when giving and receiving money. I found it to be very dignified and, in a way, humble, and enjoyed adopting the practice when shaking hands and paying for things. I got some funny looks when I got back to the UK and did not realise I was doing something rather odd.

Thai people are softly spoken on the whole; softly spoken and gentle when they use their voices and softly spoken with their body language, how they move and how they communicate. You rarely see someone waving their hands about, gesticulating, or stomping around, raising their voice or even having a public conversation on the train that is loud enough for anyone else to hear. Foreigners stand out on public transport in their ability to unwittingly include everyone in their conversation.

If by some misfortune you become *'jy rorn'* (hot-hearted) and lose your cool, causing you to do any of the above (except perhaps loud talking on the train – that is just embarrassing) then you will damage relationships, usually forever. It is difficult for us foreigners and we learnt the hard way when still living with a family in Sivilai, early on in our time in Thailand. We walked round to the church one day to find our host cutting down a beautiful tree in the church compound. We were horrified. Trees provide much needed shade in a hot country, especially in somewhere like a church compound where people gather together. Looking back, our language ability was far worse than we realised, and we really never understood why he was doing it. He could have had a very good reason. But we lost our cool, raised our voices, gesticulated and I think even committed a totally unforgivable sin by calling him a fool. He lost face big time and as a result our relationship was never the same again. He never showed it when we lived with his family – but he was the driving force behind trying to get rid of us on more than one occasion over the next seven years, and his animosity was probably rooted in his loss of face because we raised our voices in a demonstration of anger directed at him. So, keeping cool, speaking softly, not showing overt emotion of any kind, moving gracefully and of course smiling are what Thai people are so good at and value highly.

And yet – when a Thai person picks up a microphone or has access to an amplification system there is a complete metamorphosis. Any event where there is the opportunity for amplification of sound calls for loudspeakers, floor to ceiling. And everyone wants to have a go with the microphone – whether to sing or tell jokes or just speak loudly! Parties, weddings, funerals, merit making, concerts, funfairs, evangelistic rallies, Christmas and any other public gathering – all require noise. There is no concept of noise pollution and noise goes on all night. In Sivilai most people go to bed at about 8 pm; the town is deserted and other than the odd TV it is very quiet. Except for when there is a party or any of the above – or movie night.

When we were there, every month a traveling cinema would come to town. They would set up a huge screen in a field and whole families would turn up with their mats and cushions and food and drink and literally watch movies from sundown to sunrise – even on a school/work night. The volume was so loud we could often hear the music, and sometimes even the dialogue, from our house on the other side of the village. Our house literally shook as the dinosaurs stamped their way through Jurassic Park.

On one occasion our neighbours had a merit-making ceremony and they showed movies for the community as part of it. This time the screen was outside our gate and people sat in the church grounds to watch. We tried to go to bed but the screen was very close to our window. Not only did the house shake all night, but we were horrified to discover that after midnight they were showing nonstop horror or porn. Thankfully most of the children were curled up asleep by then, but it still makes you wonder what effect it has on relationships for pornography to be so openly shown for all at a community event.

It is not only on the nights when events happen that villages are noisy. When Sue, a friend from Chiang Mai, came to stay she was horrified at how noisy village life is – especially early in the morning. First, anyone who believes that cockerels crow at dawn is seriously misguided. Our experience is that no one has taught Isaan cockerels how to tell the time and they are likely to crow very loudly at any time from midnight onwards. Living next to a cockfighting establishment meant that we became experts on this. Also dogs. They do not sleep at night. Or at least Sivilai dogs do not, especially when there is a full moon. The screaming, howling and barking at night, at certain times of the month, was enough to keep the soundest of sleepers awake. Graeme, a regular visitor, finally invested in a slingshot in order to try to get a good night's sleep!

It was not only the animals that disturbed Sue and other visitors. About twenty yards from our house was the main speaker for the headman's amplification system through which he communicated with the whole village – very loudly at 5.30 am every day. He would get everyone awake and ready by playing loud music which, amazingly, we learnt to sleep through. It was, however, impossible to sleep through his alternative wakeup call: Isaan stand-up comedy. Once he was sure everyone's complete attention was focused on the noise coming from the speaker, the day's announcements would begin. There were no local newspapers, and in fact few people in the villages read any kind of newspaper. So all national and local news was passed on through these morning broadcasts, with the headman's political bias of course. Then there was the lost-and-found section of his message. On the day Sue was staying she seemed very perplexed at breakfast. Sue speaks Thai and what she had heard him say was that three bananas were missing,

33

two grey and one brown. What she did not realise was that the Thai word for 'banana' is very similar to the Isaan word for 'buffalo'!

Sivilai Hospital was very proud of its ninety-nine per cent uptake of infant vaccinations. The reason, I am sure, for this great success rate was pure shame. The day of the vaccinations the announcements were long – the name of every child due to be vaccinated was read out, and then if they failed to go to the hospital it was read again, every morning until they got the shots. No self-respecting parent would be repeatedly humiliated unnecessarily!

Every year Thais celebrate the Buddhist festival of *Loy Kratong*. Chiang Mai does everything bigger, louder and longer than anywhere else in Thailand. Loy Kratong lasts a day in the rest of the country and is not even a public holiday. In Chiang Mai it lasts at least four days and I do not think anyone could possibly work having not slept for four nights! The reason for the lack of sleep is that it is like living in a war zone. Constant fire crackers, as loud as grenade explosions. Fireworks of every shape and description. Bangs that shake the house and make you jump out of your skin every other second and wonder if your ears will ever be the same again. And then there are the music and microphones, amplifiers and throbbing bass non-stop for what seems like days and nights – continuous vibrating noise! Yes, it is extraordinary, eardrum-shattering, deafening fun and I cannot imagine a Thai festival being celebrated in any other way!

CHAPTER THREE

Pets, Farm Animals and Wildlife

Early on in our relationship Mike and I realised we were both dog people. Whilst we were in Bangkok doing language study we were given

a puppy from a litter of mutts up our street. *Namtan* in Thai – meaning 'sugar' or 'brown', which he was – or Danny, as he was more often called, was a faithful friend for several years. He used to deliver messages between us and one of the Sivilai elders, who would carefully write notes and stick them in his collar and send him home. He was a classic con artist with lovely puppy-dog eyes, who would go round the homes of congregation members convincing them that he had not been fed. His favourite game was to follow behind a big frog or toad patting the ground hard behind it with his paw to make it jump. Inevitably he would eventually misjudge where to pat and actually kill the poor creature. You would then see him getting more and more frustrated because it would no longer jump!

Soon after we arrived in Sivilai, Lady also came on the scene. She was a beautiful Thai ridgeback and very agile. It was a while before we realised that she was spending her days climbing the ladders up into traditional Thai houses and making herself comfortable on other

35

people's beds! After her first litter of puppies we decided one was enough. I recently found letters written to ask people in the UK if it was OK to inject her with human contraceptives, as we had no other contraception available. I don't know if they answered, but that is what we did and it worked! Mee was an interesting dog to look at – a stocky white Laos mountain dog with a short stump-like tail. We had her when Rachel was a toddler and on several occasions they were found eating out of the same bowl. Mee's main claim to fame was that when she got ill and clearly knew she was going to die, she went into the church and lay in front of the cross to do so!

Sivilai was a fairly dangerous place to be a dog. Tharae is a small town about sixty miles away and is almost entirely made up of a community of Vietnamese Catholics. I visited regularly because one of the convents held eye clinics to which I took truckloads of patients. Its other claim to fame was the dog market. Many Vietnamese see dog meat as a speciality and this particular market only sold dog meat. About once a month, every dog in Sivilai would start to howl and before long the truck from Tharae would appear with cages on the back, full of screaming animals. We would rush to lock ours up to keep them safe. The driver insisted they would never steal a dog, they always paid – two plastic buckets per creature! We were never tempted and in fact regularly locked up any dogs that were around, as well as our own, in order to keep them safe. The Karen, amongst whom we worked in Sangklaburi, also eat dog and, according to our friends, black dogs are the most delicious. When Zorro, our big handsome black dog, disappeared from Sangklaburi the year after we moved to Bangkok, we couldn't help wondering about his fate.

In Bangkok stray dogs are very common. Many run wild in the small back lanes of the city known as *sois*. So, stray dogs are known as *soi* dogs. They are everywhere and incidences of bites from rabid dogs are higher in the capital than anywhere else in the country. The Soi Dog

Society attracts an amazing amount of support, particularly from the expat population. Their goals are admirable. They do not necessarily catch and find homes for the dogs. They catch them (and cats) and sterilise them to prevent further proliferation of the dog population, and then put them back on the streets. I can't help wondering what method they use. When we lived in rural Sivilai one of the more unusual sideline jobs that Mike, the minister, took on was to provide a castration service for the local dogs. On a home leave to Scotland a kindly vet gave him two sets of castrators – one for small animals and another for the big bulls. They are like huge pliers that you use to crush the lines and blood supply to the testicles – bloodless and, although excruciatingly painful, fast – ten seconds a side! It is not surprising many Sivilai dogs either crossed the road when they saw him coming or growled menacingly!

Living in the countryside means that it's a good idea to have cats as well as dogs, to keep the mice and other pests away. Surprisingly though, we often found cats to be frightened of the pests rather than to be predators. On one occasion I came downstairs into our kitchen to hear a strange noise coming from the top shelf of our food cupboard. Food cupboards are usually a metal structure with mesh sides and glass front in the top section. They are designed to keep pests, including ants, out whilst maintaining air flow. Somehow a very large mouse or small rat had got trapped in the top of this particular cupboard. Unfortunately for her, just as I realised what the problem was, our kitten walked into the room, so without thinking twice I threw her into the cupboard and shut the door. It was hilarious – a little like watching a washing machine spin as the two of them chased each other round and round a very small space. After quite a struggle the kitten won the day and was rewarded for her efforts.

Later cats proved themselves useless at catching mice and rats so we had to resort to traps. The normal kind was a cage-type trap, which leaves one with a very much alive trapped rat. We decided that if the cats couldn't deal with them then the dogs should learn. We would shake the cage around to daze the rat and then release it, allowing the dogs the chance to try to catch and kill it. They turned out to be much more efficient hunters than any cat – and they didn't play with their prey, just snapped the neck and killed it immediately. Eventually they were fast enough so that we did not need to shake the cage first!

The other common way of catching rats, and in my opinion much crueller, is to put down a cardboard mat covered in very sticky glue. Once the rat is stuck there is no escape. The problem is the glue is not fussy about what it catches. On Aylie's fourth birthday, a kind church member gave her a cute kitten in a gift-wrapped box with a ribbon. The trauma of being unwrapped and cuddled by an enthusiastic four-year-old sent the kitten running for cover under a cupboard. The next thing we knew she was screaming and on investigation we found her lying on her side completely stuck to the rat glue. She had to be cut off and then we had to clean her up. We started with water – useless. Then talcum powder – also useless. At that point I had to go out and left her in the hands of the two traumatised children and our good friend Kristen – who is a genius and thought to try vegetable oil. Eventually all the glue was off, but the kitten remained greasy for a long time.

Of course, another way to deal with a rat is to bash it on the head. You have to be pretty fast to get it though. One night in Sangklaburi I came face to face with a rat in the bedroom. I started to chase it around the room, not unlike the kitten in the cupboard and, I suspect, I was being quite noisy about it. The next thing I knew my neighbour ran up the stairs into the house and flew through the bedroom door armed with a massive iron pipe. He was convinced I was being attacked by an intruder or, if not, then at least a deadly snake. People laughed about me and the rat for a long time!

One does expect rats in the countryside and on the whole they are well fed in the fields, seem quite clean and healthy, and are not that interested in invading homes. In contrast, city sewer rats are dirty, disease-ridden and more disgusting – and there are a lot of them, some enormous, to be seen scurrying along the gutters on the streets of Bangkok. My worst rat memory in Bangkok is of rats running up and down the rows hunting for popcorn in the cinema when Mike and I first started going out together. Not romantic!

Although our cats were never good with rats, one of them, Cleo, proved herself to be a hunter. Every day we would come downstairs in our house in Bangkok to find cockroaches littered all over the floor. Before we got Cleo we used to pay an exterminator to come in once a month, but after we realised how gifted she was we stopped our subscription. However, she had a funny quirk which was not very pleasant. She liked to post cockroach corpses into shoes. Mike was the one who suffered the most from this as he never left his shoes outside on the rack like rest of us. (He had to sit down to remove lace ups, rather than kicking off sandals or flip flops at the door and he was lazy about putting them away!) The other person who became a victim of Cleo's cockroach disposal was my mother who, on arriving back in the UK from a visit to Bangkok, removed her shoe to reveal a much squashed cockroach corpse – smuggled through customs unawares.

The first time we drove to Sangklaburi in 2000 there was great excitement as we passed a pickup truck with two horses in the back. The children had never seen a horse in Thailand; it was something they had always dreamt of seeing. For them elephants were the norm, not horses!

Since an early age elephants were a part of their lives. In Sivilai the touring elephants would come to the village every six months or so to put on a show of football playing, dancing and delicately stepping over the willing volunteers who would lie in their path. I was always terrified, as at least once a year a tragic accident involving a tourist and an elephant's misplaced foot would hit national headlines. In Sangklaburi the elephants we often saw on the road with their mahouts[8] were working, on their way to pull logs or take tourists for rides. Occasionally we would see them in the wild. Often we would come across elephant dung on the forest roads, estimate how old it was by how moist it appeared and so work out how far away the creatures were. Elephants are not the only animals with whom we have had encounters, although probably the biggest.

During the floods in 2011 crocodiles got a lot of publicity. Thailand has hundreds of crocodile farms. Some have shows attached to them and attract bloodthirsty tourists thrilled by the crazy trainers sticking their heads between the enormous jaws. The main reason crocs are bred in Thailand is for the worldwide handbag industry. The reason they

---

[8] a person who works with and rides an elephant

were in the news in 2011 is because the disastrous floods in Thailand meant that thousands of them escaped from said farms and were on the loose terrorising flood victims. Looking back through our newsletters written for friends and supporters (called *Fish Wrapper*) this was the third time we had reported crocodiles on the loose but in 2011 it was on an unprecedented scale. One man required a hundred stitches after meeting a croc in his neighbourhood. Many others were bitten by snakes flooded out of their holes and looking for a dry place to stay.

Snakes, or the threat of meeting snakes, were a major part of our lives when we lived upcountry. We often had them in our garden and occasionally our house. I hate them and would always leave it to someone else to deal with them. Zorro, our big black dog in Sangklaburi, was a fantastic snake alarm; he could see them from a hundred yards or more away and he had a special bark to alert us to the presence of danger. He used the same bark for scorpions. Occasionally he would have a mental lapse and we would rush over to find him barking at a frog – but on the whole he got it right. Once, when we lived in Sivilai and Rachel was a toddler, Mike was away and I met a poisonous snake in my kitchen. Of course my protective maternal instincts kicked in and I could not just run and hide screaming for help, which would have been my normal response. My immediate, slightly off-the-wall reaction was to put on Wellington boots before bludgeoning it with the broom! I guess I thought my bare feet were more vulnerable than anywhere else if I missed the first time and just made the thing angry! It must have been quite a sight.

Whenever we travelled to Udon from Sivilai for presbytery meetings, Mike and I would stay with our good friends Jim and Joan on their farm. The journey took about five hours on the motorbike on dusty or muddy roads, depending on the time of the year. I loved the long drives and would often read a whole book or take cat naps on the back of the bike. However, we would arrive sweaty and exhausted, looking forward to the chance to relax and get cool. The house was more Western than ours with fewer opportunities for livestock to get in. We enjoyed the luxury of air conditioning and would often sit working at the desk in our bedroom. One day, Mike was working when he heard a plop, as a lump of poo landed on the desk. He looked up to see a long snake tail hanging down from the air conditioner. The air-con company men were duly called and in fear and trepidation they extracted two snakes from the machine; they must have crawled in through the vents from the large bamboo stand against the wall of the house. We went to bed that night confident that we were safe, as they had also blocked the hole. What we did not know until years later was that the next day, when Joan was sweeping the room after our departure, she came across the third member of that particular snake family hiding behind the dresser, where it had been all night!

Thailand has many smaller critters, most of which are completely harmless. It becomes second nature to tip shoes upside down before putting them on. A scorpion sting on the toe is not nice. Neither is the experience of sticking your foot into a toad! The most frightening-looking scorpions are big[9] and black. They are, in fact, the least worrying as they are so visible and would send both Danny and Zorro into a complete frenzy of barking to warn us of their presence. The far nastier ones, that managed to sting both Mike and Aylie several times, are small and brown and hide in dark places under things like boxes or logs. Interestingly, their experience is that you should never put water on a scorpion sting or it just makes it like an electric shock. The best cure is potato or onion rubbed in and a good dose of conventional analgesia.

Centipedes are even nastier than scorpions. They are big – up to twenty centimetres long, and bright red or orange, so you would not expect to miss them. They are also fearless and move very fast. Kids love them because if you chop their heads off they keep moving for a long time afterwards – great sport! Mike's centipede experience was not fun. He was ploughing a field – we had an 'iron buffalo', a mechanised tractor you walk behind – when somehow a centipede got down inside his boot and bit him. It was agony but he was alone and a long way from home. Eventually he managed to drive his motorbike back to town, where the hospital gave him local anaesthetic and blocked the feeling in his whole leg!

---

[9] about ten centimetres long

Other insects that are a nuisance are the ants and mosquitoes. Ants are everywhere and you soon accept their presence and learn which ones to ignore and which ones to get rid of. Woe betide anyone who leaves a crumb of food on the kitchen counter or, worse still, makes the mistake of snacking in bed! But it is not just food that attracts ants. In the dry season they are desperate for water and there is a particularly nasty tiny black ant that has learnt that damp towels are the cosiest place to hang out and drink – and maybe get a nice meaty meal if some daft human makes the mistake of rubbing themselves with said towel! White towels may seem crazy in a country of dust and mud, but they were the only ones for me, because you have some chance of spotting the little biters before they bite you. Much like checking shoes for scorpions (and frogs), always check your towel for ants! Then there is another type of ant that wants to escape the water in the rainy season. One night, Mike and I were tucked up in bed on our mattress on the floor, in our wooden house on stilts in Udon, when we were aware that the floor was moving. We ran down the stairs to find armies of ants climbing the pillars of our house and up inside, making themselves at home where it was dry. We tried everything: throwing water from above; spraying the pillars with pesticide at the base. I have no idea how we got rid of them in the end; all I can remember is that we never made it back to bed that night.

One of the things I missed when we moved to Bangkok was the nightly experience of sleeping under a mosquito net. We lived in a sealed city house with proper windows and without the threat of malaria, so mosquito nets were not deemed necessary. In the countryside in both Sivilai and Sangklaburi, it was a different story. Each night the net would be unrolled and tucked under the mattress to protect us from mosquitos and the diseases they carry. There is something wonderfully secure and comforting about being in this net cocoon, well tucked in and shielded from anything 'nasty' out there. When we slept on a mattress on the floor, nets protected us from cockroaches and four-legged vermin as well as the obvious mosquitoes, spiders and other flying creatures. A net also protects from lizard poo that drops from the ceiling! However not all mosquitoes come out at night. The ones with the stripy legs, which can cause dengue fever, are daytime mosquitoes. Having succumbed several times, I realise that either my eyesight or my reflex reactions are clearly not good enough, or I would have spotted them before they had the audacity to bite me.

Not all flying bugs bite, but they can still be an incredible nuisance. Our house in Sivilai was not screened and so, on what we called 'buggy' nights, we really suffered. Even with the screens in Sangklaburi they would still find a way in. Flying ant-type insects, known as 'drunk bugs' in Thai, are attracted by the lights and would swarm around them. The only way to stop it happening was to sit in complete darkness. We had many a night when we ate bug-covered food. Bug-infested spaghetti is particularly memorable. One way to help get rid of some of them is to put big bowls of water under the lights. The bugs are then attracted to the reflection and drown. People were appalled to discover that we then threw them away – most of our neighbours were very excited by buggy nights as it meant an easy way to catch a special protein addition to their evening meal. One of our poor visitors had a terrible experience. He was reading in bed with his mosquito net up when the bugs came. For some reason he then put the net down and so was trapped inside with a swarm of big flying termites. His screams could be heard from a long way off – stuff of horror films and nightmares – but in our insensitive way we thought it was hilarious!

Lizard poo is particularly smelly and unpleasant. However, in my opinion, lizards are our friends. They eat the mosquitoes and so I am more than happy to have them in my home. There are the small little ones – *chinchuk* in Thai and gecko in English. They are cute and hide behind pictures on the wall. They make a chirping noise and kids love to play with them because when you grab them by the tail it just comes off in your hand and they grow another. Dookays are much bigger and look rather like dinosaurs or mini dragons with green skin and orange florescent spots. They sing loudly making a noise from which they get their name *'doo-kay'*. Many people seem to be afraid of them but I find their presence comforting – unless you mess with them. Apparently if they do bite you have to break their jaws to get them off. We had one in the bathroom for months and I was quite sad one day when, cleaning my teeth, I stepped backwards and missed standing on its corpse on the floor by a hair's breadth. Obviously the cat had had a fun night.

Dookays can move deceptively fast. I discovered that one night whilst trying to prevent one from eating some defenceless house guests we had. One morning a child who lived next door yelled up for us to go and look at his latest find. We got outside to find three baby owls at the bottom of a tree. One had died already but the other two were alive and distressed. We left them for a while to see if the mother would appear but no big owls showed up. So we took them home and suddenly had babies to feed – often and with bugs (they liked them alive) and mice or rats. I horrified my mum when I confessed that we had caught and killed a rat and were keeping it in the fridge alongside our fresh food. Click and Clack, as we called the owls, were incredibly trusting and tame. They would strut around the house and, despite the fact that they were only six inches tall, you would think they owned the place. Until the night I heard a big rumpus and went out to find them being stalked by a dookay. They were not so confident then. Eventually they learnt to fly and we kept them in a cage-like room attached to the house, which they could get out of if they wanted, but gave them protection from predators. One day we noticed a big owl in a nearby tree, the next day they were gone – we hope to a family reunion.

Owls were not the only birds we had dealings with. Several of our church members raised chickens and ducks, and we became dab hands at vaccinating chicks! On one night we were participating in a Bible study when there was a massive storm. The Bible study host was raising chicks on a big scale for a chicken company and somehow they got wet – about three hundred of them! The study was abandoned and we had to borrow every towel and hairdryer that we could find in the village to dry them before they died of hypothermia.

Cockfighting is very common in north-east Thailand and taken very seriously. Men spend hours grooming their birds and in some cases care for them better than their own children. Huge amounts of money change hands as bets are placed on the winners of the fights. The local cockfighting arena in Sivilai was next door to the church and their regular meeting time was a Sunday morning. The church's main reason for investing in an amplification system was in order to override the noise from the excited gamblers and cockerel owners. It was a huge relief to the congregation, and recognised as an answer to prayer, when the land owner decided to sell up and the church was able to buy the plot. We built a nursery school, which was probably just as noisy and disruptive but not on a Sunday morning!

We saw various other forms of animal life taking residence in our house or garden in addition to the dogs, cats and creepy crawlies. Animals featured as part of the many agricultural development projects over the years, particularly cows, buffalo, chickens and goats. With no form of veterinary or agricultural training we learnt as we went along.

Two of the projects, already going in Sivilai when we arrived and supported by the national church department of development and social welfare, were a cow and buffalo bank. The banks provided the members of the project with two fully mature breeding female animals which they looked after. This is intensive work as the way people raise cows and buffaloes is to have someone with them all day roaming around the countryside looking for grass. They then breed from the animals, using a bull provided by the bank and sharing his services with all the 'member animals', and raise the calves. After four years the initial animals are returned to the bank plus half the number of calves, now grown, which are passed on to other people. The project member keeps the other calves they have raised. It's a good system. However, when we arrived we walked into a massive dispute.

A cow had died and the people raising it had buried it without getting it checked over. There were strict rules about who is responsible for an animal if it dies; they are meant to get all the appropriate vaccinations etc. and if they don't then those raising the animal are responsible. If it can be proved they have done everything to keep an animal healthy but it dies anyway then the buffalo/cow bank bears the cost. Leaders in the church believed the family had not done all they should have and that the animal had died unnaturally. So they demanded that it be exhumed to check it over. I can't remember all the details but I think in the end it was found to have died of anthrax and then a decision had to be made about whether or not the family was liable. All very stressful and difficult when you are just getting to know people and don't know the first thing about farm animals. We certainly did not want to be accused of taking sides. And yet – God provided. Into the middle of all of this walked two young vets from Scotland. We didn't know them and I have no recollection of how they found us – but they camped down on the floor and not only helped sort out this dispute, but did routine health checks on all the other livestock. Perfect timing and one of many examples of the right people appearing when needed.

When we moved to Sangklaburi we once again got involved in raising cows. We had seven beautiful creatures and a huge bull – which resulted in a few cute calves. Most of the time looking after them was fairly straightforward. One morning, however, when Mike was away, one of our neighbours came running into the schoolroom where I was teaching the girls, screaming for help. The whole community followed him to the field where we found that a cow had fallen down a wide-mouthed well. It wasn't a deep well but the cow was well and truly stuck and not happy. We pulled and shoved to no avail and eventually Sompong, who was pretty scrawny, managed to get down underneath the struggling cow and, miraculously, push her up enough for everyone else to pull her out. Sadly, we were all too involved to secure any photographic record of the dramatic event. Sometime after we moved to Bangkok, Rachel was heard to comment on how boring life was; no cows falling down wells in the city to brighten up the day!

Being a long way from an urban centre there were no vets in the area so we had to do all we could to keep the livestock healthy. The first essential was to build a crush, or holding gate, so that they could be treated without risk of people being kicked or trampled. Ours was the first crush ever seen in Sangklaburi and Mike spent hours poring over the book 'Where There is No Animal Doctor' and on the phone to Peter, one of the authors, getting advice. In the end the crush worked brilliantly and was the envy of other farmers in the community. I was very grateful for it as I administered treatment to cows! Animal medicines were not available either – and hefty cows and bulls need a much bigger dose of most things than a human. I remember giving antibiotic injections to a cow and having to open about twenty ampoules to get a big enough dose before injecting into its massive backside. On another occasion the bull was severely dehydrated and needed intravenous fluids. Putting a drip up on a bull is not the same as a human, and my colleague and friend Doe and I combined our efforts to do it, receiving instructions from Bob, a missionary vet, directing operations via phone from the other side of the country. Another interesting way of administering drugs, which Mike managed better than I did, is via a spray up the cow's nose. Suffice to say they do not like it much!

A spray up the cow's nose.

Taking bovine rectal temperatures was a new skill we acquired. It is important to tie a long piece of string to the thermometer before inserting it, or it could get very lost up the back end of a cow! The children found it fascinating to learn what the normal body temperatures of different animals are – not something I think kids in the UK do in a practical science lesson! A cow's normal temperature is 38.6°C but a calf's is 39.2°C. Goats take the prize though; their normal temperature is 40°C.

'Baebae' is my written approximation of the sound a Thai-speaking goat makes, and it was one of Rachel's first words. Bottle-feeding kids was something I always thought would be a soothing, gentle, almost romantic occupation. However, when we bred goats, I discovered that they are incredibly demanding. Our first litter of kids in Sivilai was born out on the co-operative farm Mike had set up about three miles from the village. They seemed to eat constantly and I recently found a photo of me feeding three at once. I can't remember why their mother didn't feed them herself! It got so time-consuming we ended up moving them all to our house, which is why Rachel heard them calling out morning, noon and night, and mimicked them.

Breeding goats was experimental in the area and our plan was to provide a cheap alternative meat. However, billy[10] goats have a very strong smell and flavour which we knew people would not like – unless they are castrated. Sadly, my first effort at castration with a scalpel ended up in the goat almost bleeding to death. I got so desperate I jumped on the back of the motorbike with it and took it to the hospital. By the time we got there the bleeding had almost stopped and amazingly the kid survived, but the hospital staff teased me about it for a long time! It was after that incident that our friendly vet in Edinburgh gave us the castrators which were used on goats as well as dogs – no incisions required.

Of course, if you want to breed goats you need one good 'one hundred per cent male' billy as well as the nannies. Ours was a huge creature who was incredibly strong and stubborn. He lived out on the farm and had to be kept tethered with a long rope or he would run away. In fact, the rope ended up not being strong enough and one day he disappeared. We searched far and wide and eventually found him a few days later caught up in a bush near the river. He had pulled so hard on the rope that it had cut into his neck and by the time we found him the wound was full of maggots. Once again we, the self-taught vets, were treating an animal with help from a book. He had to have the wound thoroughly cleaned out with hydrogen peroxide – obviously a job for a nurse, according to my squeamish husband – and then powder put in each day. It was a logistic nightmare as the only way to keep him still was a rope around his neck. Somehow he survived and fathered several litters of kids.

It was at Easter time that we fed our congregation their first goat – massaman curry style. It was surprisingly popular and became a church tradition for Easter in Sivilai. In Sangklaburi we didn't raise goats but

---

[10] male

there was a big goat farm outside town – a business selling the goat meat to a cannery in southern Thailand for consumption by the large Muslim population. One of my friend Doe's jobs on the side was to vaccinate them for the owner, so we had connections and were able to buy one of the flock for an Easter feast. We collected her the day before and locked her in our outside, not often used, bathroom. However, a church member decided to use the bathroom and the opportunistic goat ran for her life. And did she run! Moses, a visitor who had popped in to see us, chased her all around the town, through the school, through the market and for miles around, to the amusement of many onlookers. Eventually he caught her and carried her back, only to have her escape again! On the third attempt she was caught and put in lockdown. One would like to think that plucky goat earned a reprieve from the pot – but no. She made a delicious massaman curry.

CHAPTER FOUR

Finding New Ways to Celebrate

Easter falls during the hottest time of year in Thailand. Traditionally, this was when the missionaries would retreat to the cool of the hills, or the beach. As a result, many churches in Thailand have never really celebrated the death and resurrection of Jesus, or have just taken on some of the more Western traditions, without ever having much understanding of what it is all about. We tried to spend time teaching the significance of Lent, holy week and the events of Easter day. For a young church that has come out of a Buddhist context (ninety-six per cent of the population) with no Judeo-Christian background, the concept of Christ's sacrifice is a hard one. There is no understanding of propitiation of sin through sacrifice. In fact, there is very little concept of guilt either. It is a shame society. Very simplistically explained, it does not really matter what you do unless you get caught and are therefore shamed So, explaining the meaning of the cross has to start from a completely different angle than talking about Jesus taking on the guilt of our sin and dying in our place, most of which means nothing to someone with a Buddhist background.

A few months after we moved to Sivilai a motorbike mechanic called Sam became a Christian. He was very excited about this new life-giving relationship he had with Christ and all it involved, entering into everything with enormous enthusiasm. One of the church traditions for many years had been that everyone went to clean up the graveyard early on Easter morning. This was particularly special in Sivilai because the Christian graveyard was actually a donated section of the Buddhist monastery grounds. Cleaning up and holding a worship service there on Easter day was an important part of the Christian witness in the village. Sam was so looking forward to his first Easter. He had planned that we would not only have a worship service, but also act out that first Easter morning in the graveyard.

Sam was so excited that he did not get to sleep until very late. We  were surprised when he didn't turn up at 5.30 am with everyone else, but we all got busy cutting down the dense undergrowth and wielding our hoes and machetes in an effort to tidy up generally. Suddenly, as it started to get light, a voice came from high up in the trees. It was Sam, shouting, 'Why do you look for the living amongst the dead? He is not here. He is risen!' He had overslept. On arrival at the graveyard he had im-mediately climbed a tree in his pyjamas and a pair of wellies and the first thing we knew of his presence was this voice. Of course, everyone fell about laughing and then we started to sing and worship. It was an unforgettable Easter morning!

Another tradition the church had established before our arrival was an Easter egg hunt in the church grounds. There was no chocolate involved. They would look for and then eat together a picnic breakfast of hard-boiled eggs. This was a huge treat for everyone and they thought it was very odd that we got excited about chocolate eggs sent to us from the UK. In our latter years in Sivilai the youth group had a lot of fun in our kitchen dying the eggs with bright florescent food colouring on Easter Saturday for the Sunday hunt. Some of the old people in particular thought nothing of munching their way through four or five eggs, just because they were available and there was a fun party spirit about it!

In Sangklaburi our small local church did not have a graveyard to clean. However, we did have a most spectacular view of the rising sun over the lake. Each year the church would build a bamboo structure and cover it with grey-painted cloth to represent the empty tomb, and we would gather on the hill to worship together as the sun rose on Easter morning.

One year I preached about Mary meeting Jesus in the garden and not recognising him through her tears. As we read the story together, with the mist drifting off the lake and the birds singing their dawn chorus, the scent of the beautiful tropical flowers and the hazy pink light, it felt like we had been transported back to that garden on the first Easter morning.

Easter Sunday morning worship in Sathorn Church in Bangkok, where we were members for a couple of years, was different again. I don't actually remember worship as such; just a lot of fun. The church property includes a four-storey building with balconies on each floor. Every Easter the church family would gather at dawn and people would compete to see who could throw a raw egg off the fourth-floor balcony and have it land without breaking. There were some incredibly imaginative inventions: parachutes of every description; eggs wrapped in layers of bubble wrap; eggs in the middle of cushions and soft toys. But there were a lot of broken eggs on the car park below!

Feet in Thailand are considered to be very dirty. You should never point your feet at anyone, or step over anything, or touch anything with your feet, or use toes to turn something on, like a fan, or pick something up. You would certainly never touch someone else's feet by choice.

So, to introduce foot washing at a Maundy Thursday communion service was completely radical. Also, in a society where age hierarchy is very important and the younger always pays respect to the older, it is unheard of for an older person or someone in a position of leadership to kneel before a younger person, let alone wash their feet. Jesus washing the disciples' feet, as recounted in John 13, seemed to take on far more significance in our small rural church communities: for 'rural feet' read 'dirty feet'!

One year when we were in Sangklaburi there was a most amazing electrical storm. All the power went off and so the Maundy Thursday communion and foot washing service was held with everyone huddled around a few candles in the corner of the church, to stop the wind blowing them out. There was a deeper, richer meaning to the foot washing and sharing communion as the gales blew around us and we concentrated in the darkness on serving one another in such a profound and meaningful way.

———————

Christmas has always been the big celebration for the Thai church, in contrast to Easter. Even though most rural Thais have no idea of their own birthday and never celebrate it, the church (probably again through the influence of the early missionaries) has made the birth of Christ the highlight of the Christian calendar. It is very different from Christmas celebrations in the West, because it is an entirely communal event. No families shut away in their homes gorging themselves in front of the Queen's speech. 25th December is a normal working day, unless it happens to fall on a weekend. So, churches all choose their own date to celebrate, any time in the month of December. Not only does this mean they can pick a weekend when people are free, but it also means Christians spend the month of December travelling around celebrating Christmas in each other's churches! It is really one long party. The Karen actually call it 'Sweet December' and launch the month with a watchnight Sweet December service at midnight on 30th November.

Christmas is expensive. So from 1st December groups of carol singers – the Karen have particularly beautiful voices – go around singing, usually all night, to raise funds for their Christmas celebrations. They specifically sing outside homes where Christians live and you are expected to get up and listen, providing snacks and money, whatever time it is. The singing is, as I have said, beautiful, but after a few 4 am wake-up calls it gets a little wearisome.

In Bangkok, for our last two years we lived in a student centre. One night in December every year, the students who live there also sing carols late into the night around the city. Our last Christmas in Bangkok they piled into our small flat, about forty of them, singing beautifully, accompanied by guitars, flute and recorder. Once they had sung they made themselves at home, stuffing themselves with cookies and cake, looking around the flat, flicking through our books, chatting, laughing and relaxing. Before they left they prayed for us and I had to hold back the tears. The same thing had happened just a couple of hours before when about twenty office staff from the CCT had come to sing. Their prayer for us after the carols was so loving and caring, I felt overwhelmed. It made me realise afresh how much we were a part of the family there.

The reason Christmas in the countryside is expensive, and so the carol singers need to raise money, is that it is the church's opportunity to reach out to the whole community and host a massive party. Our first Christmas upcountry in 1991 was a roller coaster experience. We wrote about it in letters and our regular newsletter, the *Fish Wrapper:*

> *Here in Sivilai Christmas Day was 29 December. It all started the day before with about a hundred people coming to the church to make baskets full of delicious sweets out of sticky rice, kidney beans and banana, wrapped in banana leaves and steamed. Groups of ladies sitting on mats on the floor telling stories as they skilfully made the mouth-watering little packages of sticky sweetness. There were church members and their Buddhist neighbours and friends working together and talking about the meaning behind the big party. We presumed the sweets were to be eaten on Christmas Day – but by evening we were surprised to discover they had already all been consumed – not one was left. At 3 am on Christmas morning the men of the church came to slaughter the cow that had been waiting patiently under our bedroom window, in order to feed everyone. From about six the church was full of women preparing breakfast (for the whole community) and getting the kids' make-up on for the nativity – which they promptly rubbed off when they ate their breakfast. The service eventually started and the church was packed. Traditionally all the village comes along to any celebration regardless of whose faith it is. It is a wonderful evangelistic opportunity. We had to compete with the noisy cockfighting arena next door as usual, but for once we were probably louder! Everyone was trying to keep warm as it has been unusually cold and rainy since the middle of*

the month. After feeding lunch to about 500 people we played all sorts of games – three-legged races, sack races, pass the parcel with about 90 kids and 20 adults, all afternoon. Quite exhausting, considering we had been up since the small hours.

The evening meeting was a combination of a carol service with songs, readings and a sermon and a cabaret with many different dances and songs of all sorts. By the time it finished people were wrapped up in blankets and ready for the films we had ordered. When we changed the second reel at 11.30 pm I turned the lights on and looked around and everyone was asleep. So we turned the projector off and went to bed! All in all it was a great way to celebrate. It was exciting in the weeks before to tell the Christmas story to those who had never heard it and see them get excited. However, the day itself was not without its frustrations. Despite talking about preparing for weeks, no one actually did anything until a few days before when they bought the cow. We felt everyone had expectations of what Christmas should be and expected us to be able to read their minds and by some magic fulfil their expectations – without being told what they were. When we did things in a different way they were disappointed. This lack of communication is not uncommon but was really highlighted over Christmas.

The subsequent Christmases in Sivilai were less stressful for us, as we learnt to be more laid back and made it clear we were not responsible for everything that did or did not happen. 1994 was particularly memorable as it was Rachel's first Christmas, and Mike's parents were with us, as well as our best man, Graeme. They coped admirably with the butchering of a pig, a cow and several chickens outside their window in the small hours. Lying in bed, I listened to the screaming pig, followed by hours of chopping with heavy knives on tree trunk boards, as the pork was minced for the traditional Isaan dish, *laap*. Mincing a whole pig by dawn takes noisy dedication.

Sangklaburi Christmases also had a community focus. Galilee Church, on the compound where we lived, had a particularly sporty feel to its celebrations. Christmas Day began at 7 am each year with a three-mile run. Mike ran and I drove the follow-up car, picking up stragglers. It was amazing how many of the runners did it in flip flops or even bare feet. As everywhere in rural Thailand, the church community produced constant food for hundreds: big steaming pots of curry and rice served on tables and benches made especially for the occasion out of bamboo. The morning service was always a long affair with lots of different choirs singing and a sermon, usually in Karen, Thai and Burmese.

Sketches, dances, songs...

As soon as lunch had been served and consumed, then the tournaments began. Teams came from as far as fifty miles away to compete in volleyball and *takraw*[11] competitions and everyone took it very seriously as there were money prizes. One of the more imaginative games for the 'not so seriously sporty' was a sort of relay race for mums

---

[11] cane ball

and grannies, which involved threading a needle before running back! There was more food in the form of an evening meal; then a service from the main stage constructed in the middle of the compound followed by the evening's entertainment. Sketches, dances, songs… Everyone joined in and about a thousand people came to watch, wrapped in blankets and sitting on mats on the ground. Many years later Rachel wrote a poem for school in the style of Seamus Heaney, describing the year when, aged about seven, she prepared to perform.

Crying at Christmas

Excitement and electricity pulsed through the cool dusk
Breeze, sending brightly coloured streamers and balloons
Bobbing. The sweltering heat of day was vanquished,
Replaced by a rare chill. Bobble hats and jackets
Appeared as the crowd settled down, buzzing and chattering,
The festive spirit shining out of all their faces.
Mats are rolled out as yesterday's squealing Christmas pig
Is shared in steaming bowls of curry.
The stars twinkled above as carols blared from speakers
Around the field, mixed with the croaks of frogs
And the melodious hum of crickets.
Babies lay slumbering, contented on laps,
Oblivious to the bustle around them. My sister sat on
Nanny's lap, her eyes straining to stay open,
Her head tipping backwards and forwards. The stage
Went up, torches balanced precariously as spotlights.
Behind the curtain of bamboo the first few acts
Waited nervously, prepping and preening for their
   five minutes
Of fame. I stand among them, my dance rehearsed and
Music ready in my hand.

Every flick and turn, kick and step practised
And memorised. No visitor to our house escaped
Without a private recital, no neighbour was denied a
Preview performance. I peered out from
Behind the makeshift scaffold and gaped at

The sea of staring faces. My hands shook and my stomach
Turned. Two tears trickled down my face, followed
By a torrent more. Gripped by an unfamiliar new
Feeling, my sobbing grew uncontrollable and even
The efforts of the Virgin Mary from the first act
Could not comfort me. For the first time, I was scared.
I could not go out onto the stage.

Rachel Fucella, 2009

This makeshift stage and people-covered field is in stark contrast to the Christmas night dinners we enjoyed in Bangkok with Sathorn Church. Every year on 25th December they hold a Chinese banquet. The church car park is transformed and two hundred tables set, seating ten per table. The exotic dishes appear course after course, accompanied by non-stop entertainment from the stage: carol singing, nativity plays, rock bands, opera singers and some years a famous pop star or two. There was huge excitement as the prizes were handed out, a couple between each act, to those whose seat numbers corresponded to the ones drawn by Santa from a hat. We always hoped to win the fridge or a fan, but the best we ever got was a tea set for four! It was a lot of fun, and not a turkey, roast potato or mince pie in sight!

Christmas decorations in Bangkok appear early. By the end of November you start to see blue Christmas trees, purple reindeer and many different-coloured stars, and Santa Clauses outside malls and office blocks. The shopping malls play Jingle Bells incessantly. Every building tries to outdo the others with its garish decorations which completely miss the real meaning of Christmas. However, where we lived, at the Student Christian Centre, they have been using the same decorations for nearly fifty years. They are the most beautiful star lanterns. The frame is made of bamboo, and the bamboo is re-covered each year with butcher's paper. It is a massive job and the whole basketball court is covered with mats on which groups of people work with paper and glue to make these magical lights. It is harder than it looks as sticky fingers catch on the thin paper and fix it in the wrong position! The Centre is blessed with many huge leafy trees and somehow, with the help of tall bamboo ladders and miles and miles of electrical extension cords, the lanterns are hung from the trees, appearing as hundreds of stars. They are visible from the elevated sky train and they almost seem to point people to the cross, which is on top of the Church headquarters, the building directly behind them.

I came to treasure Christmas services at Christ Church, the English-speaking international Anglican Church, over the seven years we lived in Bangkok. The 'Carols by Candlelight' service is one of the most beautiful services of the year and was always packed. With familiar music led by an inspirational choir and musicians, the Christmas readings, and short devotions, some of which I have had the privilege of giving, it marked the beginning of Christmas for me.

Christ Church introduced me to Christmas Eve Christingle services, another of their annual traditions. Hundreds of children who never normally went to church turned up for this very special children's carol service, with as many as wanted to taking part in the nativity play. Chaos reigned, as arriving children were transformed into angels, shepherds, wise men and, if they were the chosen ones (usually the first to arrive), Mary and Joseph. And then there were the Christingles; on arrival each child received a pack containing an orange, a red ribbon, sweets on lethal cocktail sticks and a candle. They were assembled as part of the service, which ended with a candlelit procession around the church – and adults at the ready on the sidelines with buckets of water and sand! Later in the evening on Christmas Eve was the magical midnight communion service: a packed church and a real sense of reverence, wonder and awe as we greeted Jesus our Saviour and celebrated his birth. Finally, a lively, overexcited crowd of children and adults would come together for family worship and communion on Christmas morning. Few of the other international churches in Bangkok held a Christmas morning service, unless it happened to be a Sunday, and this meant many members of other churches came to Christ Church, too. Finding enough seats for everyone was a wonderful annual problem the church had!

For most people who came to Christ Church, Christmas meant personal family time, as it does in the West. Once the service was over, people usually disappeared home. However, there are inevitably those who are alone in the city or do not have the practical resources to celebrate in style. In 2011, 25th December was a Sunday and we decided to put on Christmas lunch for a hundred and fifty people. It was a wonderful occasion which required a huge amount of work. Ineke, the vicar's wife, planned it all and led the team, which comprised our family and nine young Australian volunteers as part of their three-week mission trip to Thailand. The hall was beautifully decorated and the three-course meal included all the Western Christmas favourites, such as roast turkey and ham (cured by Mike for a month), Christmas pudding and brandy sauce. There was a wonderful atmosphere and a great church family time. Most people paid for tickets and others gave tickets as gifts to those who could not otherwise have afforded it.

From very early on we tried to cook something special from our UK and US family traditions at Christmas. Mike longed for Virginia ham, so when we lived in Sivilai he started the Fucella tradition of curing our own. Almost every year he went to the fresh market and bought a pig's thigh, straight from the abattoir, so fresh it was almost twitching. Having cut the bone to size so it would fit in the bottom drawer of our fridge it was then injected with saline and soaked in a brine solution filled with spices and sugar as well as the salt. And there it sat in the bottom of our fridge for a month. For a couple of years, the local furniture maker in Sivilai, who was a member of the congregation, let us hang it in his smoke house – until the fateful year that the fat dripped on the fire and the place caught alight! When feasting time came we would boil the ham for a couple of hours and then roast it with all sorts of yummy secret ingredients on it. As well as doing our own ham, Rachel became expert at making mincemeat for mince pies and also a dab hand at Christmas cake. So, with the ham roasted and the mince pies and cake cooked, we were ready to share Christmas treats with everyone who came to our Christmas parties.

Sangklaburi is quite small and off the beaten track so there were not many expats around. However, there is a refugee camp within driving distance and so the aid workers serving it live in the town. There is also a small missionary community. The first Christmas we were there Mike was actually away visiting churches with his team, helping them with their celebrations. I did not fancy Christmas Eve with just the three of us, so we invited all the expats we could think of, and thus began the tradition of the Fucella Christmas party. That first year twenty-five people came and we feasted on roast chicken with all the trimmings, or at least substitutes for some of the more traditional ones, and of course ham. It was the first time I realised that other Westerners do not necessarily eat what my family eats on Christmas Day! From then on, we had a party every year in Thailand – usually with a carol service and communion between the main course and dessert, followed by children's games and gift exchange around the tree. Memories include squeezing about twenty people onto the roof of our house in Bangkok for an amazingly moving service under the stars and singing Frosty the Snowman at the request of one guest who confessed it was his favourite 'carol'. One year we added a twist to our gift-giving by requiring the gift to start with the first letter of the person's name. I was given a 'junky' women's magazine! Harold, our then eighty-year-old friend, was given a hat with a battery that played 'We wish you a merry Christmas' as it bobbed back and forth. For some reason he did not take it home with him and it has provided great entertainment value at our annual Christmas rituals ever since.

The most moving Christmas party was one I organised with my colleague Doe in 2004 for members of the AIDS project we had set up. About twenty-five children and adults came to our house in Sangklaburi. We served food and then a Burmese pastor gave a simple gospel message. People are not used to sermons and so happily interacted with him and asked questions. At the end, many had clearly been touched by the Holy Spirit. We were then treated to a puppet show performed by a gifted neighbour. Everyone was transfixed. The party ended with gifts all round.

What was most moving about this party was the presence of Thachii. Doe and I had been close to this twenty-three-year-old woman for three years, ever since she was diagnosed HIV positive. The first time I went to her house was quite an adventure. I had met this beautiful young lady a few days before, when she was in hospital, and had promised to visit. No one warned me that getting to her house involved climbing down a steep mountain! She laughed when I arrived, puffed out and dusty. It turned out that there was another way to get to her house that I hadn't known about which also involved a climb, but a short one, followed by a precarious balancing act to cross the creek on a bamboo raft bridge.

Visiting Thachii was always an adventure. Sometimes, if she knew I was coming, she would post her sister as look out and, when she saw me on one side of the steep-sided creek, Thachii would meet me halfway across the raft bridge and we would sit chatting with our feet dangling in the water. Over the years our friendship grew through these visits. I wish I had gone more often. I rejoiced with her when both her second husband and her healthy child were tested HIV negative, and I cried with her when her tuberculosis came back and she was once more admitted to hospital. On 30th November she accepted Jesus and asked to be baptised. She was dying. I cradled her in my arms as she was baptised and clearly declared her faith to a hospital room packed with the members of the local HIV support group, her friends. It was a very emotional night. Doe and I stayed with her late, not expecting to see her again. Her biggest regret was that she would miss the Christmas party. Well, God gave her a special gift of three more weeks of life so that she could attend the party. She was very weak and I had to carry her to and from the car, but she enjoyed every minute and was surrounded by family and friends. She died the next day.

Christmas and Easter are the two main Christian festivals celebrated in Thailand. However, there are many traditional and Buddhist festivals celebrated in every village, town and city. 'To be Thai is to be Buddhist is to be Thai.' This is a common saying and genuine belief amongst many of the majority Buddhist Thai population. So much of what happens that is a part of Thai culture has its roots in Buddhism, or more commonly, in the syncretistic mish-mash of Buddhism, Hinduism and Animism, which is closest to what most people actually practise. It makes it hard for the relatively young and minority church, especially as many of the first missionaries saw bringing their culture as almost as important as their faith, and strongly forbade converts from having anything to do with their own Thai cultural heritage.

So how does the church respond to community festivals, rituals and ceremonies that are Buddhist in their origin and an intrinsic part of everyday life for most people? Can Christians remain a part of the community and yet not take part? Should Christians avoid such festivals at all costs for fear of either becoming tainted in some way, or giving the wrong impression that they actually believe in what is being celebrated or revered? Do people see Christ's love at work if we turn our backs on what is important to them? How do we prise out the meaning of the different rituals and ceremonies, when even the people who go through them don't necessarily understand them? Can we perhaps redeem or transform them into something new that brings honour to God, and does not alienate Christians from their own culture and community? These are the issues that every Christian in Thailand has to deliberate over. These were all questions we and the church in Sivilai thought through, debated and actually tried to do something practical about. It was not theological discussion for the sake of discussion alone. It was the nitty-gritty living out of life as a follower of Christ, where most neighbours and friends held very different beliefs and practices.

As I have already mentioned, festivals are important to people. When Christians feel they cannot participate, then they become isolated within their local community. We encouraged people to get involved at a social level, including helping with food preparation, even if the festival was at the temple, in the same way as their Buddhist friends would always come and help in the kitchen at church events. We tried to help people understand that by being in the temple, their Christian faith would not be weakened as long as they themselves were secure in what they believed. The difficulty was deciding what Christians can and cannot do in terms of festival ritual.

Loy Kratong is an example of this. Loy Kratong is a water festival that happens in November, the exact date depending on the full moon. Traditionally, everyone makes floats out of banana tree trunks, although latterly styrofoam became popular and more recently I have seen very eco-friendly floats made of bread or even ice-cream cones; apparently the fish like them. Each float is decorated with flowers, incense sticks, a candle and sometimes money. Then from dusk onwards they are pushed out onto the water: rivers, lakes, the sea, swimming pools, or as in 2011, flooded roads! It is a beautiful sight with the lights bobbing on the water, and there is always a family, carnival-like atmosphere. There are two main ideas behind this practice. The first is to both thank and appease the god of water by giving the float and the money and incense on it as an offering. (I watched in amusement one year as children hid on the banks of the river downstream and jumped in to retrieve the money as the floats went by.) The second is to place one's sins on the float and send them away. This is interesting because, as I have already said, there is little concept of the feeling of guilt in what is essentially a shame-based society. But I suppose everyone is ashamed of something they have done and so people have the opportunity to feel better once a year, when they 'get rid' of their sin. Clearly Christians do not want to pay tribute to the water gods and we do not need to send our sins away; Jesus has done that for us. But everyone wants to join in the party.

Mike baptised twenty new believers in the fish pond.

One year, when we lived in Sivilai, Loy Kratong fell on a Sunday. After our morning service we all piled into any vehicle we could find – motorbikes, our truck, a cart attached to the back of Mike's 'iron buffalo' and bicycles – and headed out down the bumpy dirt road to the church farm. We continued to worship as Mike baptised twenty new believers in the muddy, leech-infested fish pond. This was followed by a picnic lunch together including barbequed fish caught in the pond. After lunch the grannies supervised and then judged a traditional *'kratong'* float-making competition – no artificial or manmade constituents allowed. As the sun set we floated our kratongs on the fish pond, whilst different people prayed: thanking God for the gift of water; confessing our abuse of water in the way we have polluted it; and praying for those suffering from drought or flood. Finally, we thanked God for what Jesus did on the cross for us in taking away our sin once and for all. It was a wonderful celebration and everyone felt a part of it. No one missed out on celebrating Loy Kratong, but God was glorified, too.In Chiang Mai not only do people float their kratong but the most beautiful paper lanterns are also released into the sky; literally thousands at a time, to the extent that the airport shuts down early over Loy Kratong for fear that the lanterns may be a danger to low-flying planes as they take off and land. A friend wrote a blog post for *Baptist Press* about the meaning of these lanterns to an ordinary woman.

> *THAILAND (BP) – I'm surrounded by thousands of suspended paper lanterns that look like glowing jellyfish in a black ocean. I reach out and touch one. It bounces off me, awaiting its ascent heavenward.*
>
> *Fireworks explode overhead. Green, red and blue sparklers provide a magical backdrop as the golden dots begin to float into the distance.*
>
> *It's easy to get swept up in the magic and beauty of the moment, forgetting the real meaning – releasing one's sin – behind this northern Thai festival called Yi Peng.*
>
> *This is my first Buddhist ceremony, even though I've traveled around the world writing stories about different cultures for years. I never knew releasing sin could seem so beautiful and awe-inspiring.*
>
> *A Thai woman standing next to me, Som Mookjai, says this is the one time of year she feels light and beautiful from the*

inside out. The 48-year-old mother of two has been practicing Buddhism her entire life and never misses this November full-moon ceremony. She literally counts down the months, and then days, until she can release her sins through these traditional lanterns.

Mookjai spends most of the year making merit, or doing good works, for her various sins and wrongdoings. She takes food to the monks, but feeding the orphans is where she finds the most joy.

"You can never do enough merit," Mookjai says as she picks up a lantern for herself and one for me.

I thank her for the gift and explain that I don't need it. My God already sacrificed for my sins. She nods, not really interested, and continues with the task at hand – preparing the lantern for launch.

Mookjai unfolds the mulberry paper, revealing a 4-foot balloon connected to a bamboo frame. She lights the fuel cell, casting a beautiful golden hue on our faces. As we wait for the lantern to fill with hot air, she prays to Buddha, asking for a year of good health.

She tells me this ceremony helps her feel comforted and brings a sense of relief. She explains that it is hard walking around for an entire year with so much on your shoulders. It makes her feel heavy. Curiosity gets the best of me and I ask how many lanterns it takes to feel total relief.

"I release lanterns just enough for my sin," Mookjai assures me, then explains that as the lanterns float higher and higher, she feels lighter and lighter. "I do not do too many, just enough for the year."

Lanterns all around us begin standing straight up; it's time for another mass release. Mookjai's lantern is ready. She places my hand on the bamboo frame to feel its gentle tug. It's ready to ascend. She whispers another prayer to Buddha and slowly releases the balloon.

We watch the beautiful lantern rise lazily, joining thousands of others in flight. They move as one in the dark sky, drifting higher and higher. When a wind current whisks the glowing mass away, we are left standing there, engulfed in darkness and empty-handed.

"I still feel heavy," Mookjai sighs. "One is not enough."

She bends down and fumbles in the dark, searching for another lantern.[12]

We were in Chiang Mai for our last Loy Kratong in Thailand. It was truly stunning watching the lanterns fill the sky and float away. We, of course, wanted to be a part of it too and so Rachel and Aylie had the idea to write a prayer on their lantern to send up as an expression of thanks to God. It was at that point that I realised that they too had understood the power of the gospel that can transform a symbol of hopelessness and heaviness into a symbol of hope in a God we can trust.

---

[12] Taken from an article by Sue Sprenkle published by Baptist Press December 16 2010
http://www.bpnews.net/34270

CHAPTER FIVE

There in the Midst

When we arrived in Sivilai we expected things to be very different from the church life we were used to, but actually much was the same. There were no pews, but they had invested in chairs, even though everyone sat on the floor in their homes and found chairs uncomfortable. They used the Thai hymnal; all translated American hymns familiar to us but often containing language no one understood. Services were traditional hymn sandwiches with a sermon in the middle. There was little if any prayer and the translation of the Thai Bible contained high language used when addressing royalty, similar to the King James version, that was often completely incomprehensible to village folk for whom Thai was already a second language. In short, the church was a representation of what most Thai people think Christianity is: a foreign religion which is fine for foreigners but not Thai. We were passionate that it should not be about a religion but more about people meeting Jesus within their own context, as relationship with Jesus is not just for foreigners but is also for Thais.

The problem was that many of the old-time Christians did not see any need to make Jesus accessible to others, to be welcoming or to reach out. They were happy to live in their own little Christian bubble and maintain the status quo. The change came when Sam was converted. He came to Christ from a background of spirit worship and living in fear. Sam and his family were known for it throughout the village. Things used to fly around their room at night; they suffered terrible nightmares and spent most of their income on appeasing the spirits and buying protective idols and amulets. When he and his family accepted Christ and were baptised, their lives were transformed. They handed over all their religious paraphernalia to the temple and they completely turned around to follow Jesus. They had no Christian background and so they hungrily consumed the Bible and teaching – and they were not afraid to question how things were done. They asked things like, 'Where in the Bible does it say we have to sit on chairs?' and, 'Why do we have to sing Western hymns we don't understand?' For a few years we did get rid of the chairs and everyone was happy on mats on the floor, but then, just as our partner churches in the West were getting rid of old pews, Sivilai church was growing and included more middle-class people not used to sitting on the floor like the farmers, so we ended up building pews!

Our friends Jim and Joan in Udon had been working on producing Christian songs to traditional local music. We tried introducing these to

worship when we moved to the church, but not being very musical found it hard. We also faced opposition from the traditionalists. Sam jumped at the idea of praising God with the tunes he had grown up with – and eventually passers-by would actually come in to have a look as they heard these same tunes lifting the roof off the church or home they were passing. Mike learnt to play the *kaen*[13] a little, and we made great drums out of ceramic fish paste jars. The tunes were catchy, and twenty or so years on I can still say the Apostles' Creed in Isaan as I sing it in my head!

As the church grew, we realised how inappropriate Western-style sermons were in rural Thailand. People are not traditionally used to listening to sermons. In temples they are

in a language, Pali, which no one understands, but it does not matter because you earn the merit just by being there. So as we preached people became fidgety and even talked to each other! The other thing

---

[13] a wind instrument made of bamboo

we noticed was that if we asked a question which at home would be considered rhetorical, here people would shout out the answer. So we abandoned the monologue-style sermons and moved instead to interactive talks or Bible studies, where we asked questions expecting response and discussion. We used a lot of visual aids too and Mike's artistic talents were called upon regularly.

We found that the prayer times surprised us. We were used to someone leading from the front or having a time of open prayer with one person speaking at a time. However there, and in many other churches in Thailand, everyone prayed out loud at once. It seemed noisy, chaotic and undignified. To begin with we reacted against it and it took us a while to get used to – but we soon realised that by doing it this way no one was put on the spot and everyone participated, because everyone was concentrating on what they wanted to say to God and not on what others were saying. People prayed from the heart because they knew only God was listening – except for the small child I once witnessed creeping around the church listening to everyone's prayers. Having initially thought it was just an awful noise, we came to see prayer times as a beautiful buzz of people communicating with their Lord. For us it was different and initially uncomfortable – but having experienced this kind of prayer, we have grown in our faith and understand prayer a little differently.

Of course, how you sit, how you pray and what you sing are fairly superficial issues, although you would not think they were superficial from the amount of controversy they caused between the old and the new Christians. There were other areas where Sam, and the many other new believers who accepted a relationship with Christ, helped us and the church think deeper about how and why we did things, in a way that had real meaning in the local context.

One thing that did not make sense to new Christians was why they had to eat 'shop-bought from the city' bread and drink imported wine – or, more often, grape juice – in order to celebrate the Lord's Supper. We could explain why Jesus used these elements as symbols: that he is the 'bread of life' and so by breaking bread we symbolise the breaking of his body; that these were the basic elements of his staple diet and therefore his 'staff of life'. But for Isaan people bread is not the staff of life and has no meaning. So fairly early on we introduced using sticky rice and water, or rosella juice made from local flowers, for communion. We met with opposition from some of the second generation Christians who did not want change. When we left the church one of the first things the older elders forced the young pastor to do was to go back to bread and fruit juice, but when we used their own 'daily bread' instead of some imported 'play food', which is how they see bread, I believe it did have a deeper meaning and helped them understand more of what the whole sacrament is about.

Throughout Thailand people use strings tied around the wrist for different religious rituals and ceremonies, many of which are linked with the occult. However, in north-east Thailand, in the area in which we lived, there is an understanding of strings which makes a lot of sense to me. People believe that everyone's soul is made up of thirty-six parts known as *kwan*. When we go through an experience of change that causes feelings of loss or grief – for example, sickness, bereavement, moving house, getting married, migrating for work – one of the kwan is frightened away and we feel unsettled and incomplete. The idea of the strings is that the whole community comes together and demonstrates their support by collectively tying strings around the person's wrist, inviting the missing kwan to return and so bring about wholeness. There are sometimes additional more occult-type practices associated with kwan ceremonies, which are unacceptable for a Christian, but the basic understanding is not in any way, I believe, evil as some have described it.

One day we were going to pray for an elderly lady, Granny Jan, who was sick. Sam, who was still a fairly new Christian, arrived with a wooden cross, over which he had draped lots of small pieces of string. We knew how some of the second generation Christians would have been taught against using strings for anything because of their 'satanic associations' and so we became quite nervous. However, we sat and listened to him explain that he understood that strings were used as a sign of the community coming together to give support to someone at a time of loss or change and bringing them back to wholeness – and surely this was as relevant for Christians as anyone else, especially as we had a God we could pray to together to ask for that wholeness. He went on to show the group from the Bible how James exhorted the elders of the church to anoint the sick with oil and pray for them. He pointed out that anointing with oil has no relevance for Isaan people – but string tying does. Together as a church community we then tied Granny's wrists in Jesus' name as a sign of our support for her and our prayers for her restoration to wholeness in Christ. Jesus was truly in the midst of us that day. A Buddhist – or more probably an animist symbol – was redeemed and transformed, and the Holy Spirit worked through it. But it wasn't just the symbol; it was the whole understanding of a community coming together to surround someone with support and care which helped our church to grow. We learnt a little more about what it means to join together as a church family to pray for someone, from a locally appropriate contextual perspective and through a practice that was alien to us foreigners.

On another occasion we were in a situation of conflict between three families who all worked together on the church cooperative farm. We met out on the farm to try to sort it out. Terrible things had been said and we had talked in circles for hours. Eventually we came to a point of resolution and agreement, but the deep hurt was still there. I realised I had some old twine in my pocket, which I produced, and we watched in amazement as the families tied each other's wrists in tears as they asked for forgiveness and prayed for each other. This powerful 'pagan' symbol had been transformed by Christ to bring healing and truth and had given us a new depth of understanding about forgiveness.

We used the strings in a number of contexts: we went to one elder's home to pray and 'tie' his son before he set off to work in Bangkok; we used them at a wedding reception to bless the newlyweds; we used them at funerals to show our support of the bereaved family. One thing we never did was to actually use them in the church. For some of the older Christians, who still held on to what they had been taught in the past, this would have been too much of a stumbling block and maybe the final straw as far as we were concerned with the very traditional legalistic presbytery leaders. We were accused of syncretism in Sivilai, but usually by people who didn't take the time to look at how God used the things that happened in the church community, which brought spiritual growth and depth of faith, pointing people towards Jesus.

Over the years we lived in Sivilai and Sangklaburi both Mike and I preached regularly in Thai, and occasionally in Sivilai we managed some Isaan. People found it funny when we used Isaan because it is a language that is looked down on, as are Isaan people themselves, so never used in any kind of educational or formal setting. However, it is the language of people's hearts and when they got over laughing they would often listen even more keenly and with a deeper understanding. New Tribes Mission even translated some of the books of the Bible into Isaan, which we introduced the church to. Again they found it hilarious because Isaan is never a written language. But many of them enjoyed reading it; a little like people in Glasgow might enjoy reading the Glaswegian Gospels. When Py came to be pastor in Sivilai, despite being Isaan himself, he had to re-learn how to preach using his mother tongue. He would never have contemplated preparing a sermon in Isaan at seminary in Bangkok. Often pastors who come from the villages but train in the city find it really hard to return to rural life, partly because of the low salaries, but I believe also because all they have learnt in the city means they often no longer fit in or understand how to communicate with their own people. I usually wrote my sermons in English but with notes in Thai of words I was not sure of. Visual aids helped a lot and after a while I think people got used to our styles and understood some of what we said.

In Sangklaburi sermons were always very long because they needed to be translated into at least one, if not two, languages. We had some people in the congregation who could only understand Thai, some who only understood Karen and some who only understood Burmese. Noi, the pastor of Galilee Church where we lived, was amazingly gifted and could switch between the three languages. We got used to preaching with translation. While what you have said is being translated, you can think about the next sentence. The problem comes if you let your mind wander and suddenly you realise everyone is waiting for you to speak and you have absolutely no idea what you last said or where you have got to! We trusted Noi to translate well. However, we were often aware of appalling translation on the occasions where English was being translated into Thai.

We ourselves were occasionally guilty of purposely mistranslating. I remember one occasion in Sivilai when we were visited by an uninvited pastor from overseas who spoke a bit of Thai and also some English which we translated. We spent the whole time praying no one would understand his Thai as we disagreed so much with what he was saying. It was at the point he was saying that hymns sung in church that did not end with amen were not true worship that we translated it as something completely different.

In Sangklaburi there was never a shortage of preachers. At least twenty members of the small congregation at Galilee Church had attended Bible school in Burma and many of them were very gifted. They were also wonderful musicians and every service would include special music from the choir, the children and the band. Music was accompanied by guitar; double bass, made out of a tea chest, stick and string; ukulele; sometimes violin; and occasionally keyboard. We did not sing many congregational hymns because it is hard to find enough that are known in all the languages. However, one of the favourite pre-worship songs that we sang every single week was 'As the Deer Pants for the Water'. Nearly all of the songs used in worship were tunes familiar to us from the West – but always sung in four-part harmony; it just seems to come naturally to the Karen.

During our time living upcountry we were constantly supported and encouraged by the congregation of the International Church in Bangkok (ICB) where we had been members during our language learning year. Occasionally we would be asked to preach when we were in the city, or specifically asked to come down and fill in for the pastor. Once we moved to Bangkok, the children and I joined Christ Church, while Mike continued attending a Thai church. From early on at Christ Church I was given opportunity to preach, which I love to do. It was so refreshing to be able to preach in English.

My first sermon at Christ Church was Easter Day. I preached at the 7.30 am service and then again at the evening service. I was the first woman to preach at Christ Church for quite some time and all seemed to go well. My dear husband maintains – in jest, I believe – that my preaching sparked what happened later that evening.[14] Something about divine judgment!

---

[14] See Chapter 6.

CHAPTER SIX

Accidents, Ambulances and Hospital Beds

On the Easter Day I had been preaching at Christ Church, I arrived home and discovered there was no water coming out of the taps. We lived in a tall four-storey town house with a flat roof. To get to the water tank involved taking a ladder to the roof and then climbing onto a platform on which sat the huge metal tank. We suspected the string was twisted that attached the float to the electric pump, so causing the water not to fill the tank, but when we got there we found the string had actually broken. Mike carefully lifted the end attached to the pump, which was connected to the power source, out of the tank and handed it to me so he could go and get more string. As he gave it to me the plastic cover protecting the wires fell off, but I did not notice. I grabbed the live end and instantly received a massive 220-volt shock which sent me into a state of tetany – where you grip even harder and cannot let go. All I can remember thinking was, 'I am going to die now.' Thankfully, Mike had enough foresight not to grab me or we would probably both have been goners. Instead he pushed me – pushed me hard enough that I let go of the live wires and landed on my bottom. But I landed literally inches from the edge of the platform, with a five-storey drop to the ground below! So – contrary to my husband's teasing, I do not believe it was divine judgment regarding what I preached about at church; I believe my angels were there protecting me!

Once Mike had pushed me he had to keep the live wire from banging on the metal tank. I was busy checking my heart and lungs were working. So he yelled really loudly for the children to come and look for the plastic cover, which had fallen down among the plants on the roof. They eventually appeared in their towels (in anticipation that we would fix the water situation), hunted around, could not find it, and left. We had played down the urgency of the situation too much in our efforts not to frighten them. So I dragged myself over to the ladder, climbed down and crawled around the roof until I found it, took it up to Mike and we both retreated. On examination I found deep burns on my right pinkie and big toe, as well as a burn on my left hand. The electric current had gone both down and across my body. Now the obvious thing to do would have been to go to the hospital but for some reason it did not even occur to me.

The next day Mike and I had to go to the bank. On the way back I got him to drop me at a coffee shop and as soon as I sat down – away from kids, I guess – the shock set in and I started to shake. It was then I realised I should go to the hospital. My doctor was furious. It was the first and only time she ever shouted at me. Fortunately, my ECG was fine, but it was a close shave and I have been regularly reminded of what happened by pain down my right side ever since. I have preached often since then and never had another incident – so I think my husband was wrong in his assessment of the situation!

We have had our share of dramatic medical events though. When we lived in Udon, Mike had his first bout of haemorrhagic dengue fever. We did not know to go to the hospital. All I knew was I needed to cool him down, so we went to a cheap, seedy resort with air con rooms rented out at an hourly rate, with piped music you could not turn off! He recovered. They say that with haemorrhagic fever it just gets worse each time you get it, so the first time is a relative doddle. A few years later Mike was admitted to hospital in Bangkok with his second experience of dengue. The day after he came out of hospital I started to feel really ill. That night, having received a cry for help from us, Mum was on a plane to Bangkok, I was admitted to hospital and Mike went back to Sivilai to welcome Py and Nip, the new pastors who arrived that week. Four-year-old Rachel taught Granny about the important places in Bangkok; I think it was the first time she had ever been to McDonalds, but the kids' play area was a great attraction.

Not only did Mike have haemorrhagic dengue fever several times but he managed to get our friend Mike Jones, infectious diseases consultant in Edinburgh, very excited. We were staying in Bangkok again when he started to get symptoms: fever, of course, but his main complaint was excruciating pain in his joints, particularly his ankles. The old Bangkok Christian Guest House, where we stayed when we were visiting the city, had no lift. Poor Mike had to crawl up and down the stairs there, and continued to have to crawl up our almost vertical ladder-style stairs in Sivilai for about three months after he was over the fever.

It turned out that Sivilai had a small outbreak of a mosquito-borne disease called Chickungunia, which is indigenous to Africa. When we got back to Edinburgh and told Dr Jones what we thought Mike had been infected with, he was very surprised and somewhat doubtful, but then reacted like an excited schoolboy when the blood results proved that Mike had indeed acquired an African disease in a rural town in north-east Thailand. Those mosquitoes must be really good at flying long distances!

My second experience of dengue haemorrhagic fever was in Sangklaburi. I was admitted to the local government hospital and Doe stayed with me most nights.[15] That same week friends of ours from South Africa were visiting, so Rags also spent a night looking after me in hospital – otherwise I would not have had the chance to see her. Not quite the holiday accommodation she had planned. I always maintain that Rachel owes her life to me being hospitalised. For a long time, she had complained of tummy ache at night and I had not really taken it seriously. When she complained to Mike of it being much worse, he brought her to see the doctor, who immediately admitted her into the room with me. The next day we were both sent by ambulance to Bangkok and by the time we got there her appendix was what the doctor described as 'almost gangrenous'. If I had just packed her off back to bed – hard, callous nurse of a mother that I am – she might not have made it in time. The local government hospital had no surgeon. Although the doctors at the Kwai River Christian Hospital (KRCH), which is about fifteen miles away from Sangklaburi, were able to do surgery, there was no facility for the use of general anaesthetic; all surgery, even major stuff, was done under a local or spinal block! We

---

[15] In a government hospital you have to bring your own caregiver.

were therefore particularly grateful to have access to a five-star-hotel-type hospital in Bangkok with fully equipped operating theatres, courtesy of our insurance company.

Mike did have one night with the threat of the knife at KRCH. Once, when we lived in Sivilai, he had to be ambulanced to Udon with kidney stones. The next time they decided to announce their presence was as he was driving from Sangklaburi to a meeting down a very bad road, but in the same village as the Christian hospital. Apparently he parked in front of the emergency room and literally fell out of the car in agony. The hospital wards were all full so he was on a bed in the corridor and most of the patients found a reason to come and look at the foreigner writhing around in pain. Phil, the doctor in charge, was keen to open him up in case it was not stones, but we resisted. I think the lack of anaesthesia was quite a big motivator in the 'wait and see' decision. His kidney stones reappeared a couple of times in Bangkok too. On one occasion a friend, Scott, had to help me carry him down the stairs to a waiting taxi to battle through the traffic to hospital. However, ER doctors were never that bothered by Mike's pain because they were always more worried about his very slow heart rate.

One morning in Sangklaburi Mike left for his daily three-mile run. About twenty minutes later he reappeared crawling up the stairs into the house with blood streaming down his face from a head wound. He was talking nonsense and when I tried to take his pulse I could not find one. Tip, a young nursing student, who was staying with us, went running off to get Doe, who, when she arrived, could not find a pulse either. Eventually we counted a heart rate of about twenty with a stethoscope. I was panicking, assuming Mike had a major head injury, which typically causes a drop in heart rate. We piled into the truck and drove as fast as I could to the Christian hospital, as I knew there were no doctors at the local government hospital. The road was really bad and it seemed to take forever.

Once we got there and he was assessed, the story came together. As he had set off on his run he twisted his ankle. The pain caused a 'vasovagal' response which made his heart rate drop dramatically, which in turn caused him to pass out, hitting his head on the railings and then the concrete floor. He had woken up in a pool of blood and crawled slowly up the stairs. The hospital identified the fact that he was in heart block and that the blood was from a scalp wound that just needed a few stitches. Another ambulance trip to Bangkok and twenty-four hours in a cardiology ICU confirmed the diagnosis and he was sent home. There was a further follow-up in the UK and a kind doctor assured me it was all OK for Mike, and if I was concerned about his very low pulse in bed at night then the answer was just not to take it!

From then on, anytime he had severe pain, his heart rate dropped from its normal forty-five or fifty down to twenty or thirty beats a minute, which is why ER docs never worried about the pain his kidney stones caused – just what it did to his heart. Eventually in 2010, when he had ended up on the bathroom floor with virtually no heart rate twice in a month, he succumbed to the pressure from the doctors and had a pacemaker put in, much to my relief. It is very frightening to not be able to find your husband's pulse.

Our other experience with an ambulance from Sangklaburi to Bangkok was also heart-related. This time it was me and my heart was going far too fast; over two hundred beats a minute for eight hours. I too lay in a bed in KRCH being observed by all the local patients before being whisked away under the instructions of our insurance company. Everyone joked that if Mike and I could only average out our heart rates we would be fine.

Aylie is the only member of the family who never required an ambulance from Sangklaburi to Bangkok. However, we did have a terrifying experience with her that resulted in a 'high speed' drive over the mountains towards Bangkok. Actually, you cannot physically drive fast on those roads but our adrenaline was pumping so it felt like high speed!

Aylie was three years old and had been with her nanny for the morning. I got home and after I had already been there about half an hour the nanny mentioned, almost in passing, that she had found Aylie drinking green stuff from a bottle in the fridge: paracetamol! I grabbed the poor child and flew to the local ER who tried to fill her with charcoal to make her sick – although I knew it was probably too late for that. At the same time, I rang our paediatrician friend at KRCH to find out how much of a dose would be dangerous – but she was out running. The doctor I spoke to did some calculations and reckoned just the equivalent of a couple of tablespoons could potentially be lethal. I had no idea how much she had taken, but a good couple of swigs could easily be that much. The thing with paracetamol poisoning is that you do not get symptoms for a few days, but if you do not treat within twenty-four hours then it is too late and you can die a painful death from liver failure.

So, we grabbed both kids – Aylie covered in black, sticky liquid charcoal – and jumped in the car and drove. I think both of us were praying constantly. Both kids cried most of the way; Aylie because of the trauma of what was being done to her for no obvious reason and Rachel because she could sense our panic and hates doing things unplanned. After forty-five miles we reached Thongphaphum, a petrol station with a bathroom and phone signals. I went to the loo, praying all the time, and Mike stayed in the car. When I came back we both said how we felt God was telling us to turn around and go home, and to trust Him. We were aware it was a terrible risk and some would think it irresponsible. We had not been able to get through to a hospital in Kanchanaburi by phone so had no idea if they had the antidote, and the treatment involves drugs down a tube in the nose every four hours for days. Very traumatic and with our uncertainty about how much she had ingested, if we had got to a hospital that stocked the antidote they would have insisted on administering it. As we made the decision with trembling hearts, the phone rang. It was our paediatrician friend back from her run. She had recalculated and reckoned Aylie would have needed to take much more than two spoonfuls for it to be dangerous, and the fact that she didn't have it running down her chin or on her clothes, and from the amount left in the bottle, we were pretty sure she had not. So we went home and Aylie was fine, although I think I held my breath for a week.

Not all of our health incidents were so 'life and death'. Some, looking back, were hilarious. Probably the funniest one involved me, a plate of red ants' eggs and a bath full of ice. Traditionally red ants' eggs are stir fried with onions and other vegetables and they actually taste quite nice. They are about the size of a Tic Tac and when you bite into them you get an acidy popping sensation – a bit like the sherbet stuff we used to eat as children that 'bursts' in your mouth. We had been treated to this feast one evening and, not long after eating, my ears, feet and hands started to itch. I knew what was coming. It had happened after eating shellfish on my first ever trip to Thailand. As I tore at my feet and hands, Mike watched in horror as his wife turned into a pig. My lips, ears, nose and other 'soft tissue' swelled enormously, making me unrecognisable. I was itching so much I didn't even think about the risk of my windpipe closing over – although it was a real possibility! All I could think of was how to stop the itching, which I reckoned meant getting very cold. Obviously I took medication but I needed more.

So we got on the motorbike and drove into the city to the home of missionaries, whom we barely knew – but did know they had a bath tub! What they thought, when they opened the front door, I dread to think, but they graciously handed over the use of their bathroom and Mike went out and bought 10kg of ice which he poured over me in the bath! I have no idea how long we stayed – until the itching stopped. But the swelling stayed with me for several days; a real reminder never to touch red ants' eggs again.

One morning in Bangkok, whilst Mike was taking the children to school, my ears, feet and hands started to itch again, with no obvious provocation. As soon as Mike got home I jumped on the bike and he sped me to the hospital. Within fifteen minutes I had been given an antihistamine intravenously. I woke up four hours later absolutely fine, having had a nice long sleep and with no piggy features at all.

CHAPTER SEVEN

Ma Gin Khao

Food is very important in Thai culture, especially at community events like festivals, weddings or funerals. In the countryside, when you walk past someone's house, the greeting they will shout out to you is, 'Have you eaten yet?' If they are eating they will shout, *'Ma gin khao!'* ('Come, eat with us!') Fellowship around food as seen in the life of Jesus, sometimes called 'table fellowship' in the West, is something that really resonates in Asia. It is where love is shown, commitments are lived out and the staff of life – whatever that might be; bread, rice – is shared.

Red ants' eggs are somewhat of a delicacy in Isaan. Other delicacies include dancing shrimp, deep fried bugs, fermented fish paste, *somtam* and laap. The little river shrimps are described as dancing because they are swallowed live and whole – dancing! They say in Isaan, people will eat anything that moves. This includes every kind of bug. Bug vendors from Isaan can be found on the streets of Bangkok and do great business. Most of the bugs are deep fried and, to be honest, I think all you taste is the oil – a bit like eating crunchy, greasy chips! It is  interesting that some 'foodies' are trying to promote the eating of bugs as a new source of sustainable protein in Europe.

Every home in Isaan has a big ceramic jar in the corner of the kitchen where the fish paste is kept. People are poor and access to protein is often limited to what you can catch yourself. In the rainy season fish are everywhere and easy to find in the streams and paddy fields. So people catch their fish and then store them in the jar with salt – half fish, half salt – and leave it to ferment. To our untrained, alien noses the stench is unbearable. But to someone from Isaan, it is the most mouthwatering aroma![16] The paste is eaten on rice or mixed in with the somtam, which is a salad made with unripe papaya, fish paste, tomatoes, lime, sugar and lots of chilli. Health educators have been trying for years to teach people to boil their fish paste before eating it – the maggots that thrive in the stuff are enough to put anyone off their dinner. Sadly, however, many do not bother and, as well as maggots, the liver fluke also found in the raw fish are responsible for one of the highest incidences of primary liver cancer in the world.

Laap is a most delicious dish made out of minced meat; chilli; raw rice that is dry fried or roasted, and then crushed into a powder which has a wonderfully nutty flavour; fish sauce; and lime. It is most commonly made from pork or duck. However, on more than one occasion we were treated to frog laap. The flavour was OK but I will never get used to the texture. The frogs are disemboweled, grilled over the charcoal and then chopped – bones and all, giving a gritty kind of feel with bits of bone that get caught between your teeth. The favourite way to eat laap in Isaan is actually as *goy*. This is the same recipe except the meat is raw. A typical lad's night out for some of the men in the congregation was to go to the abattoir at about midnight, just after the animals had been slaughtered for market, and eat beef goy together – a sign of being macho that somehow I cannot see taking off in the UK!

The most unusual delicacy we were offered was something really special. One morning a cow and her newborn calf walked past the house where we were staying. There was great excitement and the next thing we knew we were being presented with the most expensive food

---

[16] Interestingly they often react to the smell of cheese or Marmite in the way we do to fish paste.

this family would ever dream of buying: fresh calf umbilical cord, that cost a day's wages for a hundred grams!

All of these dishes are always accompanied by sticky rice. It is a special kind of rice that you steam and, when it is cooked, it is eaten with one's hands rolled up into a ball and dipped in the accompanying dish. Meals happen sitting on mats on the floor with a line of dishes and rice in baskets down the middle, alongside bundles of freshly foraged green vegetables from the fields and forests. No one needs their own plate or cutlery. Everyone just dips their balls of rice into the food. We had some wonderful Isaan meals in Sivilai – particularly together with the church family after worship on Sundays or out on the church farm.

Living with Bee and Ken for our first six months in Sivilai meant we had to eat what we were given, when they were cooking. They cooked over a charcoal stove which they only lit morning and evening. We were used to drinking coffee more often than that so we would go through the routine of boiling a kettle on the fire and filling a thermos every day. In those days no one in Sivilai really drank coffee and Bee never had. One morning she did not appear at breakfast – very unusual. Eventually when she got up she told us that she had always wondered what coffee tasted like so late the night before when we were in bed had made herself a cup. She had made it really strong and had subsequently been unable to sleep all night. On another occasion we found a group of children trying a handful of Mike's sweeteners, thinking they were some sort of sweet. They all gagged and nearly threw up! So it was not just us that struggled with other people's delicacies!

Karen food is very different from Isaan. Spices used are much more akin to those found in Indian or Burmese food with masala, cumin, tumeric and coriander used more often than the traditional Thai chillies, lemon grass and fish sauce. The Karen and Burmese dishes use beans and pulses, which the Thai tend to only use in desserts, and meals are usually eaten with ordinary rice or Indian-style chapatti. Curries are cooked with oil or ghee and will often have an inch or so of fat floating on the top.

Whilst in Isaan it was normal to hear, 'Come, eat with us!' we found that in the Karen culture the host rarely actually eats with the guest. If you are invited for a meal your host will run around serving you or sit and chat but will not eat until you are finished. It is important to remember, therefore, not to eat everything given to you, but to leave some for the family, or you will not be invited again! An exception to this was when we and our closest Karen friends had Korean barbeques together. We set a rounded metal plate over the charcoal fire and cooked our own slithers of raw chicken, pork and beef, whist boiling vegetables in the rim of the dish. I am not sure health and safety regulations would allow it in Britain – a live fire on the table and using the same cutlery to place the raw meat on and then eat the cooked food – but it is a really fun, sociable meal. On his travels Mike was frequently fed Karen delicacies which included dog, lizard and snake. Probably the most unpalatable for us foreigners is their special curry made from gibbon's intestines and the contents; it has a bitter taste and a greenish tinge!

One of my roles with Interserve, over the last few years we were in Thailand, was to provide orientation for new people coming to serve in the region. Of course, I taught them basic health guidelines including drinking bottled or boiled water and not eating food that is questionable in its cleanliness. But when offered food or drink by a host, all that has to go out of the window. When I was a child I was taught that if you are offered something you do not want, or know you will not actually be able to eat, then you should say, 'No, thank you,' and not waste good food. In Thailand and much of Asia it is the opposite. You must accept even the weirdest-looking food or dodgiest-looking water – or your host loses face. It does not matter if you actually only take a sip or tiny taste and leave the rest. It's the saving of face that is most important.

Sometimes it is also hard to accept food or drink from people because you know what a sacrifice it is for them to give it. So often the poorest of the poor are outstanding in their generosity. On one occasion I was visiting Din, an AIDS patient who had just come out of prison. She lived in one of the worst slums I have been to. Her home was actually built with brick, rather than cardboard or tin roofing as many others in the slum were, so I expected it to be OK. In fact, it was disgusting squalor. A double bed took up most of the room, with about half a metre space around it, which was piled with boxes and junk. The room was home to my friend, her adult sister, her mother, and two young nieces. Din had not been able to work and I knew they were struggling to survive – and yet, ten minutes after I arrived, one of the children came running in with the bottle of Coke she had been sent out to buy for me. On this occasion I accepted it gratefully, but then 'forgot' to drink it as I knew if it was untouched the children would enjoy it after I had left. I gave them two gifts – a special drink for the kids, but also the dignity of being allowed to serve me. Something far more valuable than the actual price of a bottle of Coke.

CHAPTER EIGHT

Prisoners, Death and Funerals

Klong Prem prison hospital is an impressive place. With its relatively new nine-storey building and its clean, light cells[17] it provides huge contrast to the overcrowded squalid conditions of most of the prisons in Thailand, including the infamous 'Bangkok Hilton'. To qualify for transfer to this hospital you have to be pretty sick. Some who reached the hospital stopped taking prescribed medication because they did not want to get better and be sent back to the normal prisons. I spent a couple of years going in once a week to visit and provide a listening ear, particularly for patients with AIDS, but others too.

Din was the room leader in the cell where most of the women with HIV and AIDS lived. Every time I went, there would be at least one person very sick or dying, even with the advent of life-prolonging anti-retroviral drugs. Some of the prisons refused to give them, so by the time prisoners got to Klong Prem hospital, their symptoms were so bad the doctors thought it was a waste of time starting them on drugs. Din was amazing. The nurses in charge of the women's building rarely went up to the cells. They would call people down to get their medication or be examined. They did no nursing care and on several occasions I had to be very pushy to get even basic pain relief for dying patients. But Din made sure people on her watch got cared for. She was very young, rough around the edges, tattooed and not someone I would want to meet on a dark back street. She spoke her mind and at times was

---

[17] wards

extremely un-Thai in her bluntness, but she really took her responsibility seriously in the way she cared for the girls in her room.

One December 1st, World AIDS Day, I was thrilled to be called on to present awards at a special hospital AIDS event. The role included giving a garland of paper flowers to Din as 'Miss ARV' for having the best improvement in her blood results over the year!

However, when I visited Din at home after her release, it broke my heart. Previously she had committed a crime, been sent to prison, discovered she had AIDS, and yet, in prison she had learned to take on responsibility. Din had people who depended on her, peers who respected her; she did not have to go anywhere or fight with bureaucracy to get her medication and she had people around her who understood what she had been through. Release from prison should have been a time of great joy... but she had no job, a mother who yelled at her, a difficult journey to get her drugs from a clinic where ex-cons were none too popular, and no hope for the future. After a while, Miss ARV gave up taking her medication. For someone with AIDS that is as good as a death sentence. Fortunately, I was able to link her up with Siam Care, a wonderful ministry to people living with HIV and AIDS, and through their friendship they were eventually able to get her back on track.

For at least one other girl I knew, the pressure was too much and she intentionally got caught committing a crime so she could go back to the security, and relative safety, of the prison hospital. I visited Nan soon after her initial release. She had been excited about getting out and even more excited when I phoned and said I would go and see her. She gave me complicated instructions as to how to find her and then said it would be too difficult, so sent a relative to meet me at the main railway station. I jumped on the back of a motorbike and after a few hundred yards we turned off the main road down a tiny alley. We dodged between people, shops, dogs, rubbish and other motorbikes, weaving left and right through what seemed like an unnavigable maze of pathways, all no more than a metre wide, lined with tightly packed wooden or cardboard houses. I would never have found the place. When we got there, Nan greeted me enthusiastically and dragged me into the small house she shared with her mother and sister. Her mother ran around getting drinks and making us comfortable. We were sitting in a tent in the room; this had been her idea to keep the mosquitoes off Nan at night. It was stiflingly hot and I thought I was going to pass out. Once everyone had got over the excitement of a foreign visitor and stopped crowding into the room or peering through the door, Nan and I were able to talk. She had prepared gifts of coloured pens for me to take back into the hospital for the girls in her cell. She missed them. Eventually, it all came out. Her mum made a living by selling cigarettes and alcohol at the railway station. Her cousins were drug dealers who worked the patch right outside the house. And they were pressuring her to take drugs again. She knew what that would do to her health. Nan had no one to turn to and no escape.

I visited regularly and tried to encourage her, but she got more and more depressed. She kept taking her medication – a sister had died of an AIDS-related illness and she did not want to die. But in the end she decided prison was better, and six months later I met her there again.

There were others who thought staying in prison was preferable to getting out, but for different reasons. The story of one woman I met in the prison intensive care unit struck me. She was glad to be in prison because of what she could do there. Jiap was in her forties, like me, and had come into the hospital from a provincial prison for an emergency operation. She had spent seven years on death row and during that time she had come to know and love Jesus. Her sentence had recently been commuted to life in prison with no chance of release. Her family lived far away and rarely visited; she had brought shame on them. When I talked to her I was struck by her joy. She seemed literally to shine. She just kept going on about how God had saved her from death in order to use her. There was not an inkling of resentment or anger about the fact that she would spend the rest of her life behind bars in terrible conditions. All she could see was what an opportunity it was to spread God's love amongst the people who needed it so badly. I am sure that God will use her mightily in the context of her suffering and incarceration, to bring many into His Kingdom. Her supernatural joy, given by the grace of God, spilt over and touched lives – including mine.

One of the people in the women's section of the hospital who was particularly encouraged by Jiap's life and testimony was Dik. She was a healthy prisoner who had been chosen from a women's jail to work as a nurse's aid in the prison hospital. She lived in the intensive care unit cell which, like all the other cells, was locked for twelve hours at night with no access for the medical or nursing staff. Dik, who was completely untrained, performed all the medical procedures, as well as providing nursing care. Soon after I started visiting she asked me how she could commit her life to Christ. What an honour to lead someone to know Jesus like that. However, it was hard; there was one Christian guard in the women's block who tried to encourage Dik, but also several who mocked her mercilessly. I met with her whenever I went in, to pray and read the Bible together. Otherwise, she was very much alone, and some of the guards and prisoners took great pleasure in making fun of her and her faith. She suffered from mild depression and we prayed for healing, which did not come. But whenever she got really low, God brought someone across her path, like Jiap, and gave her hope, peace and joy in the midst of a very hard situation.

Hope, peace and joy were hard to find in the AIDS wards in Klong Prem. They housed the truly powerless, shut away and forgotten. I could bring them very little. I could not improve their physical situation. I could not solve their problems, which were many. The seed I could sow was the seed of love, friendship and acceptance. I sat with the women and we would pass the time talking about their children, my children, the world, their stories, their hopes and aspirations. Often, in the space of just one morning, we would both laugh and cry together, and over the months I saw transformation in their lives: a hardness in some that started to melt; an acceptance of themselves, as they were accepted. I can't claim that there was a massive revival in that prison cell, but God touched lives and I believe in a small way His Kingdom was and is being built there, even though I saw no dramatic signs.

The men's section was different. Everyone there was really sick, and many dying, with little opportunity for laughing or chatting together. Most of my time on the men's ward was spent doing basic nursing care; sitting, talking softly or listening to their regrets; and holding the hands of the dying. Dying because of AIDS is bad enough, but to be dying in a prison cell away from family and friends is very hard.

I believe one of the roles of Christians in circumstances like this is to be present: present expressing love; present in practical care; present in a willingness to listen and talk, if that is what the dying person wants. When we are present, there is opportunity for Christ to transform lives.

On one occasion in the prison hospital, a Thai Christian friend from Siam Care and I had been visiting a Buddhist man regularly. He was very sick. He was a criminal. He was alone. He was dying. Usually he was asleep and latterly unconscious when we visited, and when he was awake conversations were limited and fairly superficial. However, we prayed for him, either aloud or in our hearts as we sat by his bed. *We were present.* The last day we visited him he was unconscious, clearly dying. We sat holding his hands praying. Suddenly he sat bolt upright, held his hand up and said, 'Stop worrying about me. Today I will see Jesus.' We have no idea exactly what had happened in his heart or mind, but I believe, maybe in part because of our presence on his journey to death, Jesus met him and that day he, like a criminal on a cross at Calvary, entered His presence.

It was impossible to forget that the hospital was actually a prison, with the difficult procedures to get in and out, the bars and the armed guards. But sometimes it was easy to forget the patients were actually prison inmates, to forget how the world saw them and how I would probably see them if I met them on the street. They were people whose lives had got caught up in the spiral of poverty, drugs, crime, perversions, idolatry, greed, corruption and violence; people who, society had ruled, deserved to be locked away; people whom I might have crossed the street to avoid, out of fear; people who, often out of self-preservation, had become hard and ruthless. They were criminals not unlike the ones crucified with Jesus.

The nurses on the tuberculosis (TB) ward asked me to see a certain young man because he was refusing to take his TB medication. He was only eighteen years old and was covered in tattoos from head to foot. Every bit of skin was marked with ink, including his eyelids. He was a scary sight. Throughout his teenage years he had constantly been in trouble: in and out of juvenile detention; living on the streets between stints inside. Now he was in for murder, with a life sentence, at eighteen. His eyes were hard.

I greeted him and tried to be chatty. *No response.* I asked him why he was putting his life at risk and the lives of others by not taking his medication. Still he did not respond. Eventually, after a long silence, he said there was no point in taking the drugs because he had nothing to live for. He was stuck in jail and even his own mother had rejected him and refused to have anything to do with him ever again. He was so clearly in pain and alone. I felt completely out of my depth and we sat in silence as I prayed in my heart. And then, out of nowhere, I asked him to close his eyes and pretend I was his mother and talk to me. Out came all his feelings of rejection, his shame, the pain and anger. He raged for what seemed like forever and then he sobbed like a baby, asking her to forgive him and take him back. I held him and over the next hour or so explained to him that even though his mother was not there to forgive him and hold him, there was someone who could forgive him and comfort him. I told him about Jesus and how he forgives, and then prayed with him. It was like witnessing a miracle, as he experienced God's deep forgiveness and cleansing. This kid, who was bad beyond hope in the world's eyes, really experienced Christ's forgiveness and a washing in His love.

Repentance for what he had done didn't really take place until after he experienced forgiveness, and it was a slow process. I went back to visit him often and listened to the nurses say in amazement that he was now willingly taking his TB medication. He was transformed. Justice still needed to be done. Forgiveness does not mean an escape from justice and he will still have to serve his sentence. But he has been forgiven and through it he has been healed, not from the TB, but from the inner pain that had been tormenting him. I am sure it will be an ongoing struggle for him, but he now knows he is not alone.

Not all of my conversations with prisoners were deeply spiritual. Often we talked about other things, and particularly AIDS, their medication, or how to manage the disease. Tii was a young man I visited regularly over a period of a few months. He was from north-east Thailand and was thrilled to find someone who understood where he had come from. As we talked, he told me his story. His family was poor. He had no sisters and was the youngest of five boys. As is still common in many places, his family brought him up as if he was a girl. Often, in the old days, this was the norm, as it is the youngest daughter's responsibility to care for aging parents and perform all the household duties. If there is no daughter, then a son is groomed from early childhood to fill the role, actively encouraged to dress as a women and live as a transvestite. 'Ladyboys' are part of society in Thailand, holding down respectable jobs, open about their lifestyle. Some schools even have three sets of toilets: male, female and transvestite.

Like many young people, Tii ended up coming to Bangkok to look for work. Initially he got a job in a glove factory, but the hours were long and the pay was poor. Eventually, a friend invited him to work in a bar with him in Soi Nana, one of the infamous Bangkok red-light districts. And so he started his career as a transvestite prostitute. He ended up with a two-year prison sentence because he stole a client's wallet, and whilst in prison was diagnosed as having HIV and AIDS.

When I met him he was desperate – desperate to somehow let his friends in the bar know where he was and that they should protect themselves from HIV. He claimed that no one had ever told him about HIV or that he should use condoms. He had left school after six years and his teachers clearly did not see the need to give AIDS education, or did not have the budget or understanding themselves to do it. So, together we sat and wrote a letter to his friends. It was painful, but he so wanted to warn them. He gave me detailed instructions as to where the bar was. I took my courage in my hands and headed down to Nana. It was in a very seedy entertainment complex. I found the bar and handed over the letter, but have no idea if it ever got into the right hands.

As well as writing the letter, we also made plans to go together, after he was due to be released. He wanted to actually tell his friends what unprotected sex can do. Sadly, Tii never made it back himself. He died about a month before his release date. In all likelihood, even if he had warned them, most of his friends probably did not have the luxury of choice as to whether or not to practise safe sex. So they will keep on contracting HIV and keep on dying.

––––––––––––––––

When I worked with people living with AIDS, particularly in the prison in Bangkok, where all the staff are Buddhist, I would regularly be commended for the amount of merit I must be building up by doing such good deeds. There was an assumption, which was mentioned frequently, that this must be my main motivation for coming to the prison and spending time with sick prisoners. In the world's eyes, and perhaps particularly with the Buddhist world view that says you reap what you sow and subsequently should be left to suffer, these prisoners clearly didn't deserve love. Their assumptions provided a great opportunity for me to share my faith as I tried to explain that my work was a response to what Christ had done for me, not an earning of my salvation. I tried to explain that I loved the prisoners unconditionally, because Christ loves me unconditionally. But as far as I could see, it fell on deaf ears. All I can hope is that one day my explanations and my example of loving the unlovely will strike a chord with one of them or come back to them and make sense. What it did emphasise to me is that people do not just look at what we do and who we are, they also want to make sense of our motivation.

I am sure that my motivation, even though sometimes pure and glorifying to God, was more often impure and selfish. God knows that we need constant reminders of what godly motivation is all about and provides us with little pointers as to why we do what we do. An experience with one of my patients gave me one of these very graphic and moving reminders.

God used one of the young women in the prison who had AIDS. She came into prison long before I knew her, a tough, hardened criminal. From what others told me, she was not someone I would naturally want to have anything to do with. In prison she was diagnosed HIV positive and was admitted to the hospital a year before I met her, very sick with fungal meningitis[18] which had left her with the mental age of a small child. She had become totally dependent on the other patients and at times whiny and demanding. She was both cared for and abused in the hospital, depending on the mood of the day.

This particular day she was desperately sick; in fact, I realised later that she was dying. She was skin and bone, very weak and barely able to communicate. But it was also her birthday. I had taken in a piece of chocolate cake, something she had talked about longing to eat in previous weeks, and I had persuaded the guards to allow me a small candle for it. I stood by her bed holding her hand whilst quietly singing happy birthday to her as I tried unsuccessfully to hold back the tears. Amazingly, she was able to eat a few mouthfuls of cake and as I stood

---

[18] a particularly nasty infection in the brain

by her side, slowly and gently feeding her and watching her smile, despite all her pain and suffering, I had a strong sense of the presence of Jesus. And these words came clearly into my mind: 'What you do for the least of these you do for me.'[19] It was a profoundly deep spiritual experience as I ministered to my King, Jesus Christ. What a privilege we have to be able to minister to our Saviour, as we minister in love to the suffering, the rejected, the unlovely in this world. It was a challenge too. Do I see Jesus in most of the unlovely that I meet? Is it just occasionally when the Holy Spirit moves us that we realise his presence? How can we make it the norm, and treat everyone as if we were ministering to Jesus?

The Broken Body is a book that has profoundly influenced me in my journey. Jean Vanier, who established L'Arche communities for people with learning disabilities, talks about how Jesus chose to turn the world upside-down with his kingdom values. He recognises that when we minister to those the world rejects, we meet Jesus.

If you walk with Jesus along this path,
he will lead you
to the poor, the weak, the lonely and the oppressed,
not with fear and despair,
not with feelings of guilt and helplessness,
not with anger and revolt,
not with theories and preconceived solutions,
but with a new and deeper
peace and love and hope.
And he will reveal to you the new meaning
of pain and darkness;
how joy springs
from the wounds of brokenness.
He will reveal to you
that he is hidden in
the poor, the weak, the lonely and the oppressed.[20]

---

[19] See Matthew 25:31-46.
[20] *The Broken Body;* Jean Vanier; published by Paulist Press New York (1988).

Death and funerals have been a larger part of my life than most people's. When I started working with people living with HIV, there were no drugs available and it really was palliative care I was involved with. It is an enormous privilege to get alongside people and walk with them on their last journey and from the time I worked in a children's hospice in the UK until now, I have never found it a depressing experience. Certainly, it is sad and painful at times, but it is also rewarding and fulfilling. Over the years I have recorded my experiences of journeys taken with people on the road to death, and others about funerals.

The first story I ever wrote about a death was very painful to put on paper. It was painful because I had loved Dee so much and when she died it felt like it was all hopeless and pointless.

I thought my heart was breaking. As I sat on the ground by the simple funeral pyre and watched the flames consume the coffin, the tears fell. I was not alone. The sisters of the young woman we were saying goodbye to also wept, and my tears meant we were one in our pain. She had killed herself. She had not actively taken her life, but since the day she had found out she was HIV positive she had willed herself to die. I always knew Dee was a spunky young woman who could do anything she put her mind to and she had put her mind to this. Only a few weeks before, she had come to the house early in the morning and we sat together on the swing set in the garden and she told me she wanted to die. She made the decision that she wanted to die and told me with no apology. She saw her brother suffer so much (his funeral was just three weeks earlier) that instead of fighting the disease she chose to fight life. Dee had no hope and rejected all offers of help. She actively turned her back on God and accepted that this was her karma. I had no fears that she would do something physically to take her life. There was no point in setting up some kind of suicide watch. But she had clearly decided and in a matter of weeks she faded away. As together we washed and prepared her body for the cremation, her sisters carefully did her makeup and nails, and filled her pockets with coins and bank notes so that she would have a good journey and do well in her next life. They were desperate for hope for her, even though she herself had none.

Over the next few weeks Dee's family was constantly bothered by banging doors and strange phone calls, and the monks at the temple complained that since her funeral they were disturbed by her spirit. The family eventually went to a spirit doctor who invoked Dee's spirit and her voice spoke through him telling them she was in torment. For months after her death this family suffered and found no comfort or hope in their faith or their community. And as a Christian who had loved Dee and become a part of that family, I suffered with them, especially knowing she had rejected Christ who could have given her peace.[21]

The reality of evil spirits and the power they have over people's lives in Thailand is something that I still don't claim to understand, but cannot in any way deny. Many live in constant fear and their lives revolve around appeasing the spirits through gifts and offerings, through listening to fortune tellers and prophecies and by making every decision by adhering to superstition. *Mor du*[22] make a lot of money and people live in fear of what they say. It is not surprising, when the supernatural world clearly does speak through them, as in the case of Dee's voice speaking to her family. We just have to hold on to the fact that Jesus has the victory over all of this. In fact, this is the reason many have turned to him and find the peace and security they so long for.

During the seven years in which we lived in rural north-east Thailand (Isaan) there was considerable church growth. There were many reasons for this, but one factor was an attempt by the church to find ways to be relevant to Thai people and not appear as a foreign religion. We used local music, language, symbols and rituals in worship

---

[21] *Suffering Christian Reflection on Buddhist Dukka;* article by E. Jane Fucella; editor Paul H De Neui; published by William Carey Library as part of the SEANET series.
[22] witchdoctors

and church life. Rather than starting by introducing people to Jesus the sacrificial lamb who would bring eternal life – the last thing Buddhists aiming for 'nothingness' or Nirvana want – we introduced people to Jesus the victor, Jesus the comforter and Jesus the friend. Jesus became incarnate in the lives of people where they were.

However, many new believers carried a deep-rooted concern about what Christians do with their dead. This was articulated by some villagers as the reason for not becoming a Christian. Death and the rituals associated with it are very important for Thai Buddhists. They have many felt needs associated with death and the new believers could not abandon them. They were also concerned that if they became Christians, then the religious and pastoral needs of their relatives would not be met at their funeral. It was therefore up to the small church to show that they did take death and its rituals seriously, they did want to bring comfort and hope to the bereaved, they did want to show respect to the dead, and they did want to live in the absence of fear. Christian funerals needed to show all of this, but in a new way that pointed people to Christ and did not compromise the gospel.

The funeral of Granny Jan was a good example of this. She was the matriarch of the church and was well respected in the village. As soon as she died people began to gather, bringing rice and money to help with the hospitality that would be expected over the days to come. Funerals are, like Christmas, a time when the whole community gathers, eating and staying together for several days; an opportunity both to show love to the bereaved, and to demonstrate the hope Christians find in the gospel. Granny's body was washed and dressed in her Sunday best with love and respect. Church members built the coffin and it was highly decorated with Christian symbols, as opposed to the normal symbols to frighten away the spirits. The room was filled with flowers and the coffin draped with fairy lights and a huge picture of her, not to make merit for her but to show love and respect. Each day until the burial there were worship services morning and evening using huge amplifiers, which would be the norm at a Buddhist funeral and so perfectly acceptable – a great evangelistic opportunity. One night I could hear my husband issuing a call to believe over the speaker system half a mile from our house. People stayed with the family through the nights laughing, joking and singing Christian songs to traditional music.

It was a community event and the neighbours understood that, even though what was said and done was different. There was no gambling or alcohol as there would be at a Buddhist funeral, but the neighbours still came.

There were worship services morning and evening.

On the day of the burial, church leaders came from the city, and the procession to the graveyard was a joyous event. The procession was led by the cross; then followed by the church leaders, who were robed, like monks would be; next the school band; then the coffin; and finally everyone else. There was dancing and singing to the graveyard, not to frighten the spirits or to lead the way to heaven as would be the understanding in a Buddhist funeral, but to show respect to Granny Jan, rejoice over her life and celebrate resurrection in Christ. Where the monks would normally chant there was a short eulogy, talking particularly about Granny's faith, and everyone got a printed copy of her testimony. The prayers were evangelistic too, thanking God for her life but more so for the saving power of the resurrected Jesus. Everyone was given little packages of earth wrapped in tissue paper to throw into the grave – not very environmentally friendly but allowed for participation. And at the end, sweets were thrown out into the crowd, as coins are at a Buddhist funeral, not to pay the spirit masters of the ground, as would be understood at a Buddhist funeral, but just for the fun of everyone diving for them! It was a great occasion. In fact, most of the rural Christian funerals we have been involved in over the years since then have been great occasions; real opportunities to see the gospel come alive at times of suffering in ways that are relevant and meet people's needs.

Where the church does what happened at this funeral, and actively looks for traditional symbols they can incorporate into the ritual, without compromising what Christians believe, then Buddhists notice and barriers are broken down. One Isaan pastor involved in trying to grow a contextualised church in north-east Thailand quoted villagers as saying, 'If this is what happens when Christians die, I want to die! Dying this way is great. Heaven must be more fun than even this. Those who die in God are really happy. They are not afraid.'

On one occasion I was called to the hospital to collect the body of a woman who had died. She lived in a small village where there was a new young church. She was the first Christian to die in her village. Christians had been active and present in caring for her when she was sick, even when others refused to have anything to do with her. I drove alone to the hospital to pick up her body, as the call had come in the middle of a wedding Mike was conducting in the church. All the way to the hospital I was worried about how we could arrange a Christian funeral in this predominantly Buddhist village.

We took Mrs Tom's body to her mother's house in the centre of the village. Her family knew she had AIDS. She had never been open with anyone else, but I am sure they suspected. People had been avoiding her and gossiping whenever she went by. Her daughter was not allowed to play with other children or go to school. Mrs. Tom's mother had a very basic one-room house. The walls were made entirely of planks of wood being saved to build a 'proper house'. There were no doors or windows, so during the day the family just took the planks down on one side, effectively taking away the front wall of the house. We laid her body in the middle of the room and, respectfully and gently, I helped her brother to wash and dress her, quietly explaining to him what to do and answering his questions. When we finished I looked up and was amazed. Standing in front of the house, squashed into the narrow lane, were about a hundred people – in complete silence, just watching.

When I stood up the questions started. What do Christians believe about death? Why wasn't I doing anything to keep away the *pii*[23]? Wasn't I frightened they would come after me? Can you gamble at a Christian funeral? And then, eventually, didn't I know this woman had AIDS? Why wasn't I afraid? Why did I show such love and respect?

It was an amazing opportunity to challenge people's prejudices and help them overcome their fears. The Buddhist village headman agreed to a Christian funeral and gave land for burial. The whole village came, not afraid of the dreaded disease that had killed this woman or the fact that nothing had been done to appease the spirits or make merit for her. Her daughter was accepted and cared for by members of the family who had previously rejected her, and the village allowed her to go to school. It all came too late for Mrs. Tom, who had experienced stigma and discrimination in life; but the example seen in the way the Christians cared for her when she was sick, and even in death, helped to transform attitudes in that village.

One of the roles of a funeral is to give opportunity for individuals and the community to truly realise that the deceased has gone. One funeral I attended provided a strikingly blunt illustration of this. When we lived on the Thai border many of the people I cared for came from Burma. One man had been a worker at the electricity board in his town there. He had become a Christian during his illness and when he died we arranged a Christian funeral. We were delighted to receive a message saying that some of his fellow workers from his old job would attend. As the service ended and the coffin was about to be closed and buried they stepped forward and asked for permission to speak. Much to my amazement they proceeded to read out an official document from the electricity board releasing the deceased from his work commitments, which they carefully and ceremoniously placed in the coffin. Everyone in his workplace and at that service was in no doubt that the deceased would not be going back to work and had now officially gone! Since then I have heard that this is common practice as it is believed that by

---

[23] spirits

officially dismissing the dead person, their spirit will not come back to haunt the workplace.

––––––––––––

Death is always particularly hard when children are involved. A certain child, May, had visited our home often and we could usually hear her coming as her mum, Rose, walked towards our house carrying her. For as long as I knew her, May had had trouble breathing and wheezed loudly all the time. Despite her poor health she loved coming to play with Rachel; they were the same age. Eventually, however, her lungs could take it no longer and May died.

I went to the hospital and picked her up, together with her grieving mother, father and little sister Ann, and took them the few miles home. I was not surprised when the village elders arrived. I had expected that, on hearing the news, they would come to discuss funeral arrangements at the local temple. However, I was in for a shock. They simply walked in, ignored the grieving mother, rolled May's body up in a mat and along with Mot, her father, took her away.

I went with them to a place in the forest, far outside the village, where they dug a hole and placed her body in it, filled it in and left. She had not yet celebrated her third birthday, so in their eyes was not yet fully human and so not deserving of 'proper' burial rites. Not even a marked grave. She had to be buried in the forest, because of the belief that when death is untimely the pii is unnaturally disturbed. Therefore, there is the fear that it might find its way back to bother the villagers if it is too close by.

The family was devastated and their religion provided nothing through which their personal loss and grief was recognised or comforted. In this case the love expressed by the church in their sadness eventually drew them to Christ, the great comforter. Their child was worth nothing in society's eyes, but they gained great comfort when they met the God who made that child in His own image and for whom she had great value and worth.

Not long afterwards Mike baptised Rose and her husband Mot and a few months later Mot died. Rose was one of the founding members of the support group for people with AIDS in the community which met in the church. When I spoke to her sixteen years after May died, she told me that she was the chairperson of a group of two hundred people living with HIV. She was taking treatment, which came too late for the rest of the family, and she was an active member of the church and a shining light for Christ in her village.

Another child whose life and death touched me deeply was Denju. Over the time I knew her I wrote three different short stories about her and her family, called Chasing Butterflies.

Chasing Butterflies

It was her smile which caught my attention. She didn't know I was looking at her as she watched her toddler chase a butterfly. When her child fell she couldn't run after her – she was just too breathless. The tuberculosis, which was eating away at her lungs, meant she couldn't walk more than a few feet at a time. She was twenty. So young. It made my heart break.

She lives in Burma – a country enslaved by a ruthless government with no basic structures for health care – and has rampant AIDS. Some years ago she went into hospital for an operation and was given blood. Now she is dying of the results of AIDS.

It is so hard to know how to help. When people are well enough they can cross over into Thailand for medical help and I can meet with them, encourage them and show them love. Once they get too sick to travel, once they need help the most, I am impotent. I can't go. I can't hold them. I can't walk with them on their journey.

The butterfly chasing was two months ago now. The young mum is dead. The toddler's sick dad looks after her now, but for how long?

I have started to work with a Burmese woman who can cross the border easily. Doe is a woman of compassion and she is visiting this family. As I support her, she supports them. It is early days – but maybe in the end my impotence will bring

103

about change for good – as other people catch the vision of loving those who are suffering, and as other people take on the task of walking with them in their pain. It is hard to learn to step back and not be able to help, but I am learning afresh that God never steps back. He is always there walking with those who suffer and loving those in pain.

January 2002

Chasing Butterflies 2

Three days ago, as I stood on the side of a hill next to a grave, I was caught unawares and found the tears falling. I was saying goodbye to a man I have grown to care for very much. As the coffin was lowered a butterfly hovered over the grave before flying away. Some months ago I wrote about watching Joseoo's first wife, as she watched her toddler chase butterflies. She is long dead. He has been in the hospital fighting for his life for over two months. His little three-year-old Denju has been with him, and his second wife has cared for them both devotedly. Denju has made many friends in the hospital and often comes to me to play and ask for 'sweetie money'. She will be missed – but as she becomes sick too she will be back. Church members have visited regularly and, two months before he died, Joseoo was baptised in his bed. A month ago he was well enough to go to church for the first and only time in his life and watch his wife being baptised. Despite his incredible suffering he had peace and a real relationship with Christ. As we watched him die his pain was finally lifted – but his wife's heart broke, and mine with it as I held her as she screamed. Why must people suffer so?

As I stood next to that grave I was struck by the ages of those in the graves round about – a woman of 22 in the next grave and another of 31 beyond that – and finally the grave of our dear close friend and pastor aged 49 who died not long ago. These few weeks since we returned to Thailand have been filled with such sadness. It is a privilege to be able *to share in people's pain – but it's hard. How much more can I take?*

June 2003

Chasing Butterflies 3

Denju melted the hearts of everyone she met – those big eyes, the matchstick arms and the strong grip as she clutched your hand and led you to the sweet shop. She has been part of our lives since the day I watched her chasing butterflies – a small toddler whose mother was dying and so couldn't pick her up when she fell. She was there when we buried her father and the butterflies rose from his grave. She, along with her step-mum, has encouraged and brightened the days of many who have passed through the hospital, which has been their home for the last two years. We have laughed with her and held her when she cried. We have endured her tantrums and secretly chuckled at her mischievousness. We have marvelled at her courage as she has fought this terrible disease. Now she is gone. The gap this little child filled in our world is empty. We miss her. Along with her step-mum our hearts broke when she left us. But we rejoice that this little broken hurting child is now whole. And it makes me smile as I think of her dancing with the angels.

Denju, 03/03/00-10/10/05

October 2005

Working amongst and getting alongside people living with AIDS makes you vulnerable to pain and sadness, as you see people you have grown to love suffer disease, pain, stigma, prejudice and discrimination. But it also brings joy and fulfilment as you accept them, love them, encourage them, teach them to help themselves, empower them and learn from them. This has always been my passion. Many years ago I wrote a poem about the death of one of my friends – the brother of Dee, the woman who chose not to fight HIV, whose story I told earlier in this chapter.

105

I just watched a man die
I just watched a man die.
He was young, in the prime of life.
So much to live for.
This morning he died.

I just watched a young man die.
I wasn't with him when he took his last breath
But I have held him and comforted him for painful weeks
As he screamed in agony and longed for death.

I just watched a young man die.
I walked with his family as they watched him suffer
And I mourn with them now as they grieve
And I ask, why must we watch young men die?

I just watched a young man die.
And it made me think of another woman
*   who watched a young man die.*
She watched a young man in the prime of his life
As he died in agony on a cross.

I just watched a young man die
Because Jesus, who died on that cross, but is now alive,
Has called me to walk with these young men who die
And show them Christ's love.

I just watched a young man die.
There will be more, and women too.
Help me Lord, to walk with them
*   through their journey of suffering*
And point them to you, the one who understands their pain.

February 1998

CHAPTER NINE

Getting Around

'Everything is OK now!' – wonderful words to hear but also very worrying said by a crying child, when you did not know there was a problem in the first place! These are the words I heard when I answered the phone whilst out of Bangkok attending a conference. It was eleven-year-old Rachel calling from Bangkok. Of course, I panicked immediately, but in hindsight am very grateful she didn't phone before everything was OK!

Bangkok is a very busy, noisy, crowded city of about twelve to fourteen million people, depending on whom you count! We had been living there for three months. Aylie was just six. The journey to and from school included getting the elevated 'sky train', which meant a change of trains involving going down an escalator to a different platform. Aylie has never been one to stay close – no fear and a great sense of adventure. Apparently, on this particular day Mike and Rachel did not realise she had gone ahead of them on the escalator until they got to the bottom to see two trains pulling out from the two platforms and no Aylie!

Panic set in – Aylie crying on the train when she realised she was alone, and Rachel crying over a lost sister. Mike reported it to the guards and Rachel jumped on the next train heading home – in case Aylie had gone in that direction and in the hope that she would know where to get off. In the meantime, Aylie had been rescued – going in the wrong direction, heading back to school – by a kind and thoughtful English-speaking Thai lady, who realised what had happened and took her off the train at the first station and straight to the guard. The guard had been radioed and told to look out for a lost child. So Mike was told where she was and jumped on the next train back to get her!

In the meantime, Rachel heard what had happened and was so relieved she called me in tears to tell me everything was OK. Sky train journeys after that were a breeze but we have had our share of other journey fun and games.

Night trains in Thailand are wonderful. In each second class carriage there are thirty-four seats which become bunk beds, made up by the steward with incredible efficiency and starched sheets. The lower bunks are wider than the upper ones but I discovered at great cost that the upper bunks are safer! In our younger days economising was our first priority when booking tickets, so we always travelled in the non-air-conditioned carriages. The doors and screened windows are left open all night for good air flow. It makes it noisy and smelly – but as I say, we were young! On my sister Gillie's first visit from the UK I went to Bangkok to meet her. She brought with her an eagerly anticipated new laptop computer. We had fun in Bangkok and then got the night train to Nong Khai where Mike was waiting for us – but probably more importantly for the computer. I started the night on the top bunk but then for some reason we swapped – maybe I felt Gillie would sleep better away from the noisy window. Who knows? I carefully put the computer under the pillow between me and the wall. At 4am when we stopped at a station I woke suddenly and realised that where the computer had been there was now a brand new bottle of Laos rice whiskey! All hell let loose and for the next two hours we ran around waking people up trying to find it. On arrival in Nong Khai we had to break the news to a devastated husband and do all the formalities like reporting it to the police. In the end we were pretty sure the culprit was the armed security guard on the train – so I am quite relieved I didn't wake up when he was leaning over me removing and replacing the computer.

On another occasion, very soon after we arrived in Thailand, Mike and I were on the night train, heading up to the north-east, when it was involved in a horrendous accident. A bus drove into the side of the train at an unmarked crossing. Several carriages derailed but no one was badly hurt on the train. The bus was a disaster, with many dead and injured all over the place. We were in the middle of nowhere. I have a vague memory of trying to help with the wounded in the pitch dark, but the main thing I remember is us being totally lost and eventually hitching a ride to the nearest city. We did not even really know where the city was. We never did make it to our destination.

Train rides are normally far less traumatic and usually good fun. When the girls were little we would each have a child in our bunk and so none of us would sleep much – but it was worth it for the adventure. Our last train journey was to Chiang Mai and was ruined by a very loud group of drunken tourists who ignored the steward's pleas for silence and kept the whole carriage awake until the small hours. Justice was served, however, and we all felt very smug when they were woken by the cheery steward wanting to make their beds back into seats at 6 am, and one by one they dashed for the bathroom looking very green!

One problem with sharing a carriage with so many is the ensuing sleeplessness if within the group there is a snorer. On occasions we would travel to Bangkok on the train with a group of church leaders from Udon. The moderator of the presbytery was quite a large man who had a terrible reputation for night-time noise. It was so bad that when we travelled together the person buying the tickets would always put him in a different carriage!

Buses are the most common form of long-distance public transport in Thailand. We have a rule in our family that the children always get the window seats so that they can hide behind the curtain for the entire journey, equipped with ear plugs. X-rated movies, usually horror, are routinely shown from the front of the bus with volume on full. There are occasional exceptions. The most hilarious journey I have ever made was when the movies shown were all old silent Charlie Chaplin ones – except a sound track had been dubbed on top in the local Isaan language. We were all literally rolling in the aisles laughing. I have hunted high and low for this DVD and never managed to find it. I am sure it is a collector's item!

In Thailand overnight buses vary in their level of luxury depending on whether it's a VIP bus or not. On the fancy ones, seats recline like an aeroplane seat and you even get your own personal TV screen with a selection of movies to watch or games to play. Without exception the buses stop for a meal break for both driver and passengers anytime between midnight and 2 am and everyone is unceremoniously thrown off with a coupon to buy a bowl of noodles for their midnight snack. Woe betide anyone who inadvertently wanders off or gets stuck in the loo; the bus waits for no one when it is time to leave again!

With my Thai bus experiences and expectations in mind, I was in for quite a shock when I got an overnight bus in Laos from Vientiane to the south. The first surprise was when I bought the ticket; I was asked if the person travelling was male or female. It seemed an odd question but I soon forgot about it. I was actually travelling with a young Chinese girl whom I had met for the first time that morning. We climbed the stairs to the second floor of the bus where we found beds – actually quite generous beds, slightly bigger than a bottom bunk on the train. For a moment I was excited, until we realised why they needed to check the gender of ticket-buyers. One bed was for two people! Ours was at the front of the bus and under the loud TV. My feet touched the end so I was grateful that I am so short – I have since discovered that a tall male friend, who made this journey regularly, routinely bought two tickets and even then had problems folding his body into the space! I was also grateful that my new friend was a very small Asian, thus leaving me a much larger portion of the bed than was probably my ticket's worth. Once again God's working things out for good was evident. It turned out this young woman of faith really needed a fellow Christian woman to talk to. In Laos it is hard to be open about faith and to have these conversations, especially if you are from an underground church. But she felt completely free to talk, in our very cramped conditions, under a blanket with a Laos soap opera blaring away above us!

––––––––––––––

For much of 2011, boats were the most practical form of transport in many parts of Thailand. Large expanses of central Thailand and Bangkok were under deep floodwater and boats were the only way to get around – boats made out of anything from plastic to bamboo to styrofoam to washing-up bowls. Even jet skis were used to rescue people from flooded areas and distribute emergency relief supplies. This is not the norm! However, boats were quite important at different times in our sojourn in Thailand, particularly during our time in Bangkok.

For our last two years Rachel and Aylie did their daily commute to school by canal boat. The boats are low in the water with a six-inch ledge around the edge, onto which one has to jump from the pier, and then straight down onto bench seating that goes from one side of the boat to the other. It is fairly precarious, particularly when the water levels are low and so the distance between boat and pier is greater than my legs naturally stretch! The 'boat boys and girls' zip around the boat on the ledge collecting fares, and there is quite a sense of camaraderie amongst the regular passengers. When we first moved to Bangkok in 1990 one of the members of our church youth group regularly followed the same route to school – until he contracted cholera from the polluted spray. The water is no better now, and the children saw several nasty floaters including used condoms, bloated dog corpses, and on two occasions dead bodies. The convenience and speed make the seedy side of it worthwhile.

When missionaries first established the mission hospital and school in Sangklaburi, the journey from Bangkok was much more complicated than the six-hour drive it is now. Bangkok to Saiyok was a train journey, part of which used the Death Railway built by prisoners of war in World War Two. From Saiyok it was a boat up the River Kwai, although in the dry season it was not possible to go all of the way and the last section had to be done through the jungle on the back of an elephant. It was not without risk, and one missionary was killed in a tragic boat accident on her way back to the mission station. Everything from gas cylinders to medicines for the hospital had to be transported up the river. This all changed when the dam was built and the lake filled. A good, though very windy, road was built all the way to Sangklaburi, making the journey much easier.

One of the churches Mike visited regularly from Sangklaburi is still only accessible by boat. Piloki is on the far side of the huge man-made lake on which Sangklaburi sits, with no roads to it. It is surrounded by virgin forest and the two greatest enemies of the villagers are fire and tigers. The journey from Sangklaburi is about an hour in a truck to the boat pier, and then a couple of hours in a long-tailed boat on the lake, dodging the small islands and dead trees, which are all that remain of the valley that was flooded by the building of the dam. The one time we visited as a family, we got all organised with lifejackets and drinking water and sang all the way there above the noise of the engine. What we neglected, however, was sunscreen, and we arrived burnt to a cinder and very sore.

Other boat rides on the lake were more informative or educational. Not long after we started home-schooling, Rachel was doing modules on floating and sinking in science, and fishing in geography. What better way to learn than a field trip out on the lake looking at all the different raft houses and their various floatation devices, and learning about the many and varied ways of catching fish? We even bought a fish from the market and made prints of its scales by dipping it in paint and pressing it on paper. An art class with a difference! Local history lessons were also conducted on the lake as we looked down into the water onto the tracks of the Death Railway from the Second World War, or visited the deserted temple with the watchtowers sticking up out of the water in the middle of the lake. At some times of the year the water gets so low you can actually climb out of the boat and walk around the ghostlike temple; it was the only building in the whole valley that was left standing.

When the dam was built in 1983-85, everything was relocated over the two-year period. Our house was taken down plank by plank and rebuilt. The house was Thai-style, built on stilts, and when we stood under it we could see that every plank was numbered. Apparently even the pineapple plants were dug up and replanted, and the large dookays were transported in the cage-type rat traps described earlier, and released into the new town. Families were compensated depending on the amount of land they had and the number and type of trees; a teak tree would bring in more money than a banana tree. The trees were left behind and, as would be expected, died, giving an eerie feel to the lake with its black finger-like bits of wood sticking out above the surface. There was, however, one tall palm tree that survived being flooded and towered over the lake, even when the water was at its highest, producing fruit almost thirty years on and attracting tourists by the boatload.

We have made many plane journeys over the last twenty years or so. Surprisingly we have had no particular incidents, except for almost not making it to the UK when the protestors took over the international airport in Bangkok. Sadly, we have never been upgraded to business class or collected enough air miles on one carrier to actually use them. Rachel loves to quote a well-known Christian writer in his description of economy-class seats being made for people with only one buttock!

There was an occasion, when we worked in the immigration detention centre (IDC) in 1987, when Mike had a long, convoluted conversation with one particular airline. In about 1995 we were thrilled to receive a photograph of a young dentist called Ahmed taken in his practice in Sweden. His story had been quite unusual. He had fled from his home country where he had been tortured and his life threatened on several occasions. He ended up illegally in Bangkok and, once arrested, was taken to the immigration detention centre (IDC) where we worked. He was an asylum seeker, but Thailand has not signed the UN convention on the rights of refugees, and both asylum seekers and even recognised refugees were and still are often picked up and detained in prison. Ahmed's only way out was to agree to be deported back to his country, where he knew he would be killed. So we saw him off at the airport in fear and trepidation. When he got through immigration he tore up his boarding pass and survived a few days by hanging out with tour groups as they passed through. Eventually he stole a boarding pass and somehow got on a flight to Sweden. What he didn't know was that the plane was refuelling in a country friendly with the one he was running from. When the plane landed he locked himself in the bathroom and refused to come out. When the staff found him he pushed Mike's calling card under the door. Mike was amazed to get a phone call from airline authorities in the Middle East asking what this man was doing. The miracle is that when Mike explained the story the airline took pity, despite the fact that they were likely to be fined a large sum of money on arrival in Sweden, and allowed him to continue the journey. When he arrived he was given asylum and eventually citizenship. Quite a journey of suffering, fear and uncertainty for this young man, but wonderfully, in large part due to Mike's advocacy on his behalf and the compassion of the airline staff, a happy ending.

My one other memorable experience involving air travel was a real adventure. Sangklaburi district covers an enormous area. The most far-flung place the authorities are responsible for is a small community called Jagay. It is right on the Burmese border. There is no tarmac or even concrete road to get there. In the rainy season the only way is to walk, and it can take a week. In the dry season you can drive but it takes many hours and includes about forty river crossings. As the crow flies it is only about fifty miles, but it may as well be five hundred. The border police support a small school there, and there is a health clinic with two nurses. Once a year the government hospital in Sangklaburi sends a medical team to run clinics, vaccinate children and, where necessary, pick up people who need referral to a bigger medical centre. Some members of the team drive, but two border police helicopters also transport people. I was lucky enough to be invited to go along. It was an incredible experience to fly over one of the few remaining virgin jungles in Thailand.

———————————

Should we get a car or not? What are the pros and cons? Will it set us apart from the villagers? Does it fit with simple lifestyle? Will people take advantage of it and therefore us? Will we just become the local free taxi and ambulance, or even hearse service? These were questions we asked ourselves and discussed at length with our Church of Scotland boss, John, when he came to visit us a couple of years after arriving in Sivilai. Up until then we had managed fine with a motorbike. I could not drive it; my one attempt saw me flat on my back in a pineapple field. However, Mike loved to drive the bike and I would sit on the back and read a whole novel or even sleep on the five-hour drive to presbytery meetings in the city. And yet a car was tempting. So we talked, and on John's last day had still not really reached a decision. But the talking stopped and Mike took John out to the farm for a day of hard labour.

They worked the fields, swam in the stream and ate a picnic – of food bought earlier in the market and accidentally left in plastic bags in the sun. John described it as the best day of physically hard work he had ever done. That night both John and Mike were desperately ill – fighting for the one bathroom in the home we were staying in, losing vast amounts of fluid from both ends as they 'rode the porcelain chariot' as John described it! The family they had been working with all ended up in hospital and later tests showed that John (and so presumably the rest of them) had been suffering from a form of cholera. But the next day, despite being weak and still sick, John had to travel six hours on the slow stopping-and-starting public bus to the city, in order to get a flight to Bangkok to connect with his flight home. As John sat on that bus holding his plastic bag, he turned to us and said, 'Forget all the discussions, pros and cons – *you need a car,'* and it was one of the first things he authorised on his return to Edinburgh! For a long time afterwards the church members in Sivilai gave thanks to God for His redeeming of the situation of hardship and sickness endured by John and Mike with the gift of a car! In fact, some of them had theology that stretched to saying the sickness was ordained by God in order to get us a car!

Having a car turned out to be a good thing. We never particularly felt it was abused by the village or our relationships with people changed by it. We did use the vehicles we had – a kind of estate car in  Sivilai and a pick-up truck later in Sangklaburi – to transport people and bodies, as well as pigs, goats, chickens, trees, a couple of tonnes of rice, and various other interesting things. It was definitely helpful for getting to hospital, both when we ourselves were sick and also for taking others. It was used often as a hearse. We also found having a four-wheeled vehicle, as opposed to just the motorbike, meant we were more inclined to take time off and get away and discover new places.

One memorable day trip in the pick-up actually extended inadvertently late into the night. Mike, Rachel (eight), Aylie (three), Sela (Aylie's nanny), Joanna (who was heavily pregnant), Tony (her husband), Dan (five) and Tim (a visitor) all headed off into the jungle on the Burmese border for a day of trekking and a picnic. They parked the truck as far as they could go into the jungle on the mud track at the bottom of the hill. From there they took jungle paths, swing bridges and forded rivers for the day, as well as eating their scrumptious picnic. The problems started when they returned to the truck and tried to climb back up the hill. By this time, it was raining and the dirt track had turned to deep mud. Everyone jumped into the pick-up truck and, according to Rachel, after about half an hour of revving the engine it became clear to all they were not going anywhere, apart from deeper into the mud, which was now almost to the top of the tyres. We were always organised so had two winches in the pick-up, which Mike attached to trees and tried to use to pull them out, but both broke in the efforts to get the truck out of the mud. After about three hours Tony decided to run for help – several miles. Darkness was approaching and the mosquitoes[24] were out in force. Rachel managed to slip on her back down a hill and get covered in mud and there was the beginning of panic all round.

The real panic was at home where I, having expected them back by four, was hosting visitors from Bangkok, whom we had been looking forward to having to dinner. I knew Mike would never be so late intentionally – but there were no mobile signals and no way to contact him. Eventually I rang my good friend Kristen. She worked for an NGO which had big, raised four-wheel-drive trucks, and so Kristen and Suriya, one of her drivers, went out to look for them – the heroes of the day.

By this time, Mike was sitting forlornly guarding the truck, eating left-over sandwiches, and Tony had run off into the jungle. Everyone else had found a small shelter and together they were making plans for an unexpected sleepover under the stars. Suddenly, late in the evening, out of nowhere burst forth Suriya's truck with Tony standing gallantly in the back like a chariot driver heading for the finish line. Once they reached the lonely pick-up, the extra special winch and chains under the wheels finally extracted it from the mud. They were all absolutely covered in mud, except Suriya, who directed operations, until Kristen pushed him over so that he would not be the odd one out. I got a message via their radio to their office saying all was well, and an hour later they arrived home exhausted but delighted not to be sleeping under the stars!

Suriya came to my rescue on another occasion. Mike was away and I was on standby for my neighbour, who was expecting her first baby any day. But the morning she went into the early stages of labour, I

---

[24] Mosquitoes in the border jungles carry malaria.

locked my keys in the car! I tried everything to no avail and eventually Suriya just happened to pop by. Within minutes he had unlocked the car. I have no idea how, but it made me wonder what he had done to earn a living before becoming a driver for an NGO!

My training as a nurse meant I often took people to hospital; more to be an advocate with doctors than anything else. However, being able to provide transport was a definite bonus. One of our neighbours was an elderly blind man who had moved from Burma. He lived very simply in a small shack with his wife and two sons. He spoke no Thai. One day, Angus, the missionary who lived in our house before us, got a message to say he was very sick and, could he take him to the hospital? – which he duly did. Later in the day he was going to visit and took the man's ten-year-old son with him to see his dad. The situation was very serious and Angus expected the lad to be upset. However, as they drove he became more and more concerned about the deep sighs coming from the boy and eventually stopped the car, wondering if he was about to throw up. Eventually, however, the boy explained that they were not sighs of concern for his dad, or travel sickness. They were sighs of pure joy – he had never been in a car before in his life!

The elderly man made a good recovery from the first incident, but several years later we were asked to take him to hospital. This time he had toothache. He sat in the front with Mike and despite the fact that they could not communicate verbally, Mike soon realised the old man was distressed. He thought he was about to throw up so grabbed the first receptacle he could and gave it to him. To his complete amazement his passenger put the thick blue plastic bag on his head and then pulled it down over his face and stayed like that for the rest of the journey. It is amazing he could breathe! Other drivers coming towards them almost drove off the road as they stared at this ridiculous sight, and Mike was completely perplexed. When they eventually found a translator and he asked the man what he had been doing, the man was surprised by the question. He had assumed Mike had given him the bag because he realised the distress had been caused by the cold air conditioning which was making his toothache much worse. The bag stopped the cold air reaching his tooth!

Fortunately for us, with all the travel we have done, our children have rarely been carsick. However, the twisty, mountainous road from

Sangklaburi to the next town, Thongphahum, has been known to get the better of even the strongest stomachs. On one occasion, Mike and the children were travelling, and without warning Aylie threw up everywhere. Mike did a sterling clean-up job on the side of the road and they set off again. It wasn't until they had gone another fifty miles or so that he realised her booster seat was still on the side of the road. Sadly, it was not there on the return journey. On another occasion we decided prevention was better than cure, so gave both children anti-sickness pills. The problem on that day was that I was multitasking, as usual, when I medicated them and inadvertently gave Aylie four times the appropriate dose. Luckily it had no long-term effects, but she slept for sixteen hours straight. At least she was not carsick!

When travelling on twisty roads in Thailand it is not uncommon to come across spirit houses marking the spots where accidents have happened – usually on sharp bends. About three miles before you reach Sangklaburi there is a very steep hill. The only way to go down is in first gear and it is a long way. At the bottom is a hairpin bend. One early morning I, along with Doe and all the local NGO medics who worked in the refugee camp, received urgent calls asking us to rush to the local government hospital. When we got there we found a scene of carnage. About once a month the immigration detention centre in Bangkok, where we used to work, would 'bus' Burmese illegal migrants back to the border. Mike saw them regularly when he went for his early morning run – jammed into the back of a caged ten-wheeler cattle truck. On this particular morning the truck had misjudged the hill and crashed over the barrier at the bottom, turning over on its side with a hundred and seven people in the cage on the back. The hospital team's disaster plan jumped into action with amazing efficiency and I was proud to be a part of it, but the 'red zone' for the most badly injured was the well-equipped accident and emergency department, which only had four beds – and we had about thirty severely injured people. There were mattresses everywhere including on the pavement outside. The sense of team as we worked to help these poor people was amazing and the local community rallied round – those not medical providing food and drinks for both patients and workers alike. Incredibly, only six people died, but even more astonishingly there was never any mention of this disaster in the Thai press.

On another occasion we ourselves came across a nasty accident as we drove home along the twisty road from the Kwai River Christian Hospital. Four friends on two motorbikes ahead of us had already stopped and were trying to extract the driver from the car. No ambulances with backboards and neck collars – just a group of women (Doe and Rachel were with me) hauling him out of the wreck and lifting him into the back of our truck. The injured man was not dead, but had lost the top of his skull, exposing his brain. Amazingly he did survive, at least long enough to be taken to the city. It was a traumatic experience for eight-year-old Rachel, who remembers it differently, through the eyes of a child, and recorded it vividly several years later in a poem.

Red

The red of the truck gleams in the afternoon sun,
Rays bouncing and dancing across its surface.
The rhythm of the road lulls me into a trance,
The cool breeze fluttering through my hair.
My mum, well-practised, goes carefully along
The twisting, hilly road, smoothly taking each
Turn and bend. A corner, a crowd, unusual on
This vacant road. My drowsy eyes blink open
As others clamp theirs shut, hiding faces and
Gasping out moans. A shiver down my spine.
Ominous like the motorbikes strewn by the road.
Foreboding like the hood of silver jutting out
From the roadside ditch. I feel the swerve of the truck.
The slam of doors clanging shut.
The impatience, the arrogance, the hurry.
That last, unseen twist and bend. A city man,
Unaccustomed to border roads with their pond-
Sized potholes and hazardous wildlife.
The screams swept away as the silver car
Is taken by the hills, swallowed by the ditch.
But that is not the scene before me. Just the gore,
Glass and moans before me now. My window against
His, parallel.

The red of the blood glistens in the afternoon sun,
Seeping and oozing across the surface of the wheel.
Fear is pungent, thick with thoughts of ghosts, of death,
Of memories forever ingrained. His mangled body
Pulled from the wreck, lifted into the truck. His head lulls
As he entered what might have been the great sleep.
Many claim to have seen death, it comes in many
Forms. The wreck on the hillside, the open coffin,
The burning pyre, the covered hospital bed.
These images, passing by the eyes of my eight-year-old
Self, will drive away fear in the person I am today.
I know what death looks like and I am not afraid
Because I look forward to seeing
What is beyond it.

Rachel Fucella, 2009

Off-road and four-wheel driving was one of the courses Mike chose to do in preparation for going on the mission field. It was regularly useful as he negotiated bad roads all over Thailand, and carefully maintained and fixed our pick-up truck. However, it did not prepare him for the kind of daredevil driving he had to do one dark night up a mountain.

Once again I received a phone call with the ominous words, 'It's all OK now.' It was late at night and Mike had left in the evening to travel with his friend and colleague, Rev. Chang, whose name means 'elephant' – rather appropriately, as it turns out. They were going to visit a church about a hundred and fifty miles away in the mountains on the Burmese border. I was surprised that he had arrived so quickly – and soon discovered he had not yet got there but wanted to tell someone about their near disastrous accident. They had been climbing the steep, twisty mountain road through thick forest when they were aware that ahead of them was the huge outline of the biggest bottom they had ever seen – belonging to a massive bull elephant. It was walking in front of them and did not seem bothered by their presence, so they decided to pull over and take a photograph. Mr Bull may have been happy enough to be quietly followed, but he was furious about being photographed and as soon as the flash went off he turned around and started to charge. Elephants move fast, even the big ones. Mike jolted the truck into reverse and they sped backwards down the mountain, round the bends and through the forest being chased by a very angry elephant. It is a miracle they didn't end up in a ditch or trampled, but eventually the elephant got bored and veered off into the trees. Rev. Chang and Mike were both terrified and the incident left them very shaken for the rest of their journey.

This particular area is known to have a high elephant refugee population. The deforestation in Burma drives them over the border into the still-rich forests of the national parks in these mountains. The farmers are upset because when they wander out of the forests they damage crops. To their credit, some bright business entrepreneurs have started producing *saa,* handmade paper, using elephant dung.

When Mike and Chang eventually got home the guilty photo was carefully uploaded onto the computer, never to be deleted. It is completely black but if you zoom in as far as you can and look very carefully you might just see a grey outline – which could perhaps be an elephant's bottom.

CHAPTER TEN

Whole People Make Up the Family of God

I am by nature a hands-on, practical person. It frustrates me to hear of people doing 'cold evangelism' whilst ignoring the actual physical, emotional or even spiritual realities of their listeners. If someone is physically hungry it is not good enough to just preach about the bread of life; you need to feed them too. If they are sick it is not good enough to preach about Jesus the healer; you need to both pray for healing and provide care. But, as Christians, we also need to share what we believe and whom we trust in, or we are no better than a good social worker. It is not either/or, but both/and. We should share the words of the gospel with the people we meet who have never heard of Jesus, but we have to earn the right to share what we believe within the context of relationship. When you are in real relationship with someone, you cannot isolate their soul. You have to see them as a whole person with thoughts, feelings, beliefs and needs which go way beyond what you might think you want to communicate.

So often the church seems to compartmentalise the different parts of people that make up their lives – spiritual, intellectual, physical, social, economic, emotional and psychological. We are so good at pigeonholing parts of our lives; at making things, people and issues fit into boxes. But God created us as whole people with every aspect of our lives intricately interwoven. We should not separate them. And so we firmly believe it is with ministry. We cannot, dare not, address people's spiritual needs whilst ignoring their physical, emotional, psychological, intellectual, social and economic needs. Nor should we address all these needs and ignore the spiritual.

There was an incident, which occurred when I was living in Sangklaburi, which underlined this for me and was a painful reminder that when we get it wrong, we are making a mistake that has a powerful impact on the lives of others.

When Doe and I first met Sandy[25] she was desperate. Her first husband and young child had died. Her second husband left her when their sick child was born. Her family in Burma rejected her. Alone, she was struggling to care for her young, very sick son. All she could do was hold him whilst he coughed and cried. When he was eight months old he too died of AIDS-related tuberculosis (TB). Sandy also had TB, and no one in the world to care for her. She was only twenty-three and had suffered so much pain in her short life.

As Doe and I got to know Sandy we found a bitter, hurt, angry young woman who was manipulative and a compulsive liar. She was hard to love. But love her we did. We both felt so strongly that we needed to be the hands, feet and heart of Jesus, showing practical compassion and care. Eventually, Sandy started coming to the support group near her home and gradually her defences came down and she opened up to, and became involved in, the group. Through the project's help Sandy was able to get medication for her TB and for a while her health improved. However, she needed regular hospital follow up – each visit a logistical nightmare of trying to get to the hospital in Thailand.

Late one night I received a phone call asking me to collect her from the border and take her to the hospital. She was desperately sick and eventually arrived at the border hardly able to keep upright on the back of a motorbike. The ride across the border had been along a very rough back route in order to avoid the checkpoints. There are no ambulances or doctors on call to make a home visit. I rushed Sandy to the hospital, praying as I went through yet more military checkpoints designed to keep aliens like her away, not sure that we were going to make it in

---

[25] This story of Sandy was first published in *Church Communities confronting HIV and AIDS;* ISG 44; published by SPCK.

time. I did have to stop at one point as her breathing became so bad I thought it had actually stopped.

When we arrived at the hospital it was late evening. The nurse on duty recognised Sandy. She knew her to be a difficult patient who was an expert at manipulation. She saw her as a person without citizenship and so without a right to treatment and care – and she treated her like dirt, refusing even to call the doctor to examine her. I was furious and very un-Thai in my (probably rude) insistence on admission to hospital for her. Even something as basic as a hospital bed for a dying woman has to be fought for when you are nobody – stateless and without rights.

Despite the way many had treated her, on that last admission to hospital Sandy said she wanted to be baptised. When she was asked how long she had been a Christian she replied that she had known God ever since she had known Doe and the AIDS project – because she had been loved, despite being so unlovely. Three weeks before Sandy died she was baptised. In those three weeks of living a life transformed by Christ, she touched the lives of others and died at peace.

We should have been so happy. We might even have been a little smug that she said she saw God in our love for her. But Doe and I both felt guilty and ashamed. We had known her for two years and had never explained our faith to her. She said she knew God in us, which is a fantastic thing to be told. But if we had explained our faith and introduced her to Jesus then she may have had two years of forgiveness, transformation, peace and joy, not a short three weeks. It was a hard way for us to learn the lesson. After that we continued to show practical compassion but from then on we were much better at sharing with people in words, as well as actions, about Jesus.

Holistic or integral mission is all about seeing people as whole people and reaching out to them where they believe they are – not where we judge them to be. In Sivilai and Sangklaburi we had the privilege of living amongst the people we came to serve and learning from them. That meant we were involved in every aspect of their lives: their spiritual journeys, their marriages, their sickness, their debt, their jobs, their children, their livestock, their fears, their joys and their hopes. In a small village we knew everything about everyone, whether church members or not. One of the biggest sacrifices we made was that of our privacy, as everyone knew most things about us too! We got to suffer when they suffered but we also got to celebrate with them.

When you are involved in every part of people's lives you cannot talk about spiritual matters and ignore the fact that they have no way to earn a living or access viable health care. As a result of our passion for integral mission, although we did not know that terminology at the time, we got involved in various development projects.

Mike has no agricultural training or background. He does, however, have an amazing ability to read books and actually put what he learns from them into practice. He did this when he converted an old dovecot / grain store into a house for us in England when we were first married. He did the same out on the farm in Sivilai. The church had some land which was not being used, and so Mike established a cooperative farm, with between two and four families working on it at any one time, as well as him. He spent many a day out in the fields ploughing or weeding or planting.

We grew various vegetables, chillies being the most successful. We planted trees: custard apples and bananas, bearing plenty of fruit. Our first watermelon crop was a disaster, but the second crop actually bore fruit which sold in the market. Planting pasture for the cows was a new concept for people who normally just walk with their animals, grazing them wherever they find grass. To be able to keep them in one field or even cut the grass and bring it to the cows was revolutionary. A friend came to visit a couple of times to teach us and others all about growing rice without expensive chemical fertilisers and pesticides. We spent many an hour in the kitchen grinding up neem[26] in our blender to make organic pesticide.

We joined church members in the fields, helping them plant, re-plant and harvest rice. It is back-breaking work and we were probably more there for entertainment value than any practical help – but they seemed to appreciate us making the effort. I think our physical presence with people was more important than being experts at the job. We were aware that many of them could harvest more than they needed for the

---

[26] also known as Indian lilac

family in a good year, but that if they sold the surplus locally they could not get a good price.

We joined church members in the fields.

One Christmas we embarked on a partnership adventure between Sivilai church and Zion. Zion is a large Chinese church in Bangkok where our friends Seree and Sunee are members. We had two goals: to try and get a fair price for our church members' rice and to build a relationship between two very different church communities as we celebrated Christmas together. The rice harvest happens in November and for most of November and the first half of December the whole of the downstairs of our house became a rice-packing factory. Members brought the rice they wanted to sell and we weighed each person's contribution. It was then piled up like a mountain in the middle of the floor. We spent days picking out the stones etc. and packing it in 5kg bags which were then vacuum-sealed with a special machine bought for the project.

Eventually, just before Christmas, we took a van full of church members and a pick-up truck containing two tonnes of 5kg bags of rice to Bangkok. Zion church was wonderfully welcoming and we all slept in the building. Many of their members bought rice, at a fair price, and we arranged to deliver rice to other churches in Bangkok. We joined in their Christmas celebrations. Mike's parents, Suzy and Ed, arrived for a visit in the middle of it all and joined us as we flogged rice wherever we could.

It was a wonderful experience for everyone who went, in terms of partnership as well as just the adventure of going to Bangkok. Many had never been before, and the ones who had, had gone to work on construction sites. Migrant workers often get taken direct from the village straight to the construction site. They live in tin shacks on the site and everything they need is right there. Don, one of our church members, could not understand how we could find our way around Bangkok with such ease, but get totally lost out in the rice fields!

The agricultural projects were good and some families definitely benefited. However, they were limited in the number of people they touched. One of the most successful development projects, which involved everyone in the church and was still going over twenty years later, was the credit union. In many ways it was like a savings scheme. People paid in whatever they wanted to each month (minimum 10 baht) and could then apply to borrow money at a very low interest rate. Everyone in the group had to agree to the credit union approving a loan and only a couple of people could take loans out at a time, so there was a lot of peer pressure not to default on repayments. In the six years we were involved, only one person did not pay back their loan in full and on time. In a culture where people rarely save money or plan for the future, the credit union did more than just provide money when they needed it. We ran seminars and workshops on budgeting and planning ahead. One of the biggest issues in rural Thailand is debt. People buy on credit from companies who charge enormously high interest rates: cars, fridges, fans, sewing machines; anything that would normally be unaffordable. These companies persuade people that they deserve to have these things, and they get sucked into the spiral of debt. With the open discussions that happened within the credit union meetings people actually began to realise the folly of these so-called amazing deals.

When we moved to Sangklaburi, we saw that one of the needs where we lived was a way for people to save. Those who were migrants from Burma, some for as long as three generations, did not usually have Thai citizenship. It was therefore difficult for them to open a bank account. We also noticed that although it is cheaper to buy things in large quantities, the poor often do not have enough available cash to do so. They end up buying just enough for their daily needs, and so in the long-term they spend more.

We tried to address both issues and opened the Drum Cooperative Store and Petrol Station on the property where we lived. It had always been a dream of mine to run a shop, and my dream came true. It was a steep learning curve though, as I learnt to manage inventory, shop (at MACRO, four hours' drive away), balance books and keep shareholders happy. Not to mention taking my turn at selling in the shop and pumping fuel. Sompong, one of our neighbours, did the day-to-day stuff but we worked closely together on all the administration. Members could have a certain amount of credit and so were able to afford things like a whole bottle of oil, rather than buying twenty millilitres in a plastic bag each day, which works out much more expensive. Each year we divided the profits between the members in proportion to their individual investment.

As well as helping people to save, we also wanted to stop the exodus of young people to the city. Encouraging people to stay when there is no work is, however, futile. We tried various schemes including a youth project offering their services with our tractor, ploughing people's fields, but the pull of the 'streets paved with gold' in the capital was often too much. Most of the time there was nothing we could do, but there was one occasion when we did try to get a young church member back.

Fay was the daughter of church members and the niece of several elders. She was fourteen and had gone to Bangkok to be a singer in a bar. She was beautiful. She was sending money home to support her extended family. Quite a lot of money. So, even though I am sure they knew the truth, it was easier for them to turn a blind eye and 'believe' she was just a singer. Child prostitution in Thailand is rife, with an estimated two hundred thousand children working in the sex trade. Most of them are sold or forced into it.

We found Fay in a high-class bar, dressed in a ball gown and singing on stage. A streetwise friend later told us that he would be terrified to go near the place as it is controlled by mafia-type gangs and corrupt police. We talked, although she was clearly very embarrassed that we were there. The next day we visited her in her room; we thought she would be off duty but there was a man there. When we tried to talk to her he pulled the phone line out of the wall and produced a gun. We ran.

We saw her mother later in the day who assured us Fay was happy. It turned out she had done similar work earlier in her life. We were banging our heads against a brick wall.

That Christmas Fay sent a gift of money to go towards the church celebrations, eight thousand baht. 'Dirty' money? We had no idea what to do but, amazingly, at the end of the day when the books were balanced there was eight thousand baht left!

We continued to pray for Fay. When she was eighteen she left the bar to be the 'kept minor wife' of a rich Chinese businessman. She never came home. But a few years later we did hear from her. She had become a Christian, married a foreigner who was also a Christian and was helping lead a church.

There were some young women who chose to stay in Sivilai. This was in part due to Sam's wife Jan. She is an entrepreneur and saw the need to set up a business to help young women develop a skill so they could stay in the village. So we started by organising sewing schools in the church. Each school lasted about three months. We hired a professional teacher and bought the machines, and the girls learnt to sew. Each morning we shared a Bible story and it was clear that we were Christians, but our goal was not to use it as a platform for conversion. We wanted to show love, develop relationships and give practical help to meet their felt need of not having a way to earn money.

Jan attended the first course. Soon after it finished she and I started the *Samaki* handicraft project. 'Samaki' means 'fellowship' in Thai and, interestingly, 'fish' in Swahili! Jan recruited many older women who had the traditional weaving skills, to produce the cloth on their home looms. They wove the traditional *mutmee* patterns, which are painstakingly tie-dyed into the white thread, using indigo dye. The thread is then woven and, by some miracle as far as I am concerned, the pictures emerge. Samaki became well known for its products made from the signature indigo woven cloth, which is both beautiful and practical.

The girls in the project, under Jan's management, sewed the cloth into bags. At its height the project produced over fifty different designs of purses and bags.

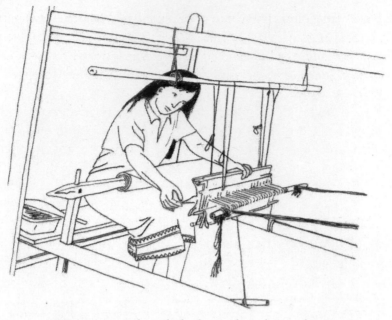

Women produced cloth on their home looms.

My roles in the project included quality control, marketing, and the business management side of things. It was wonderful to see how it took off. The project got a name amongst our partner churches in the UK for the good quality of the products, and orders poured in. Samaki handicrafts also became members of ThaiCraft, a fair trade organisation in Bangkok which organised sales and provided advice and support for grass roots projects. I, and later Jan, would travel down each month to sell the bags, and at some sales there would be a queue of people waiting to buy our stuff. Eventually the project was elected to be the OTOP[27] project for Sivilai, a government scheme promoting local businesses and projects.

Sadly, however, not everyone rejoiced in the success of the project. Some elders in the church felt that the main goal of the project should be to increase the church's finances. They wanted ownership and the right to demand payments to the church. The project already tithed ten percent of its profits to the church, but they wanted more. There was

---

[27] one town, one product

jealousy and suspicion, particularly of Jan, and little understanding of helping people outside of the church. Most of the employees were not church members and so some of the elders did not see the point. They had no understanding of integral mission or business as mission. They just wanted the money.

One of the most painful lessons we learnt in our time in Isaan was that the poor do not routinely rally round and work together to help each other. This had been our idealistic assumption. Yes, we occasionally saw incredible demonstrations of sacrificial generosity. Sadly, what we experienced was that this was a rare occurrence and more often we saw people acting out of jealousy and betrayal, willing to stab each other in the back in order to help themselves and their family. And I guess if it was me not knowing what my children were going to eat at the next meal, I might be the same.

There were some who had the same attitude about the church. They were not happy when the church grew, from about twenty members to a hundred and fifty over seven years. They did not want to share their resources, and they did not want to change. They did not have a vision to reach out and draw others in. When development projects worked, their main goal seemed to be purely to add cash to the church coffers.

I think part of the reason for this runs deep in Thai culture. I may well be wrong but our reflections, experiences and observations have led us to believe that Thai culture is often introspective. This may be tied in with Thai nationalism and pride in the Thai identity. The way we have seen its outworking is similar at local, national and international levels. So, for example, we noticed that during the various wars and disasters that we saw covered by Thai media over the twenty-two years we were there, the news was almost always reported entirely from the perspective of how it would affect Thai people. This was particularly obvious during the Iraq wars, where most reports just focused on the plight of the small number of Thai migrant workers there.

At a local church level, we noticed the lack of intercessory prayer even in large, established churches, and when it did happen it was almost always for things affecting members of the church; rarely for the wider world. In fact, most village people in those days had little concept of the wider world. Television has changed that now, but many still feel no need to be interested or care for a world that has nothing to do with them. At a national church level Thailand has sent very few people to be missionaries into other countries or cultures. There are capable people and in some parts of the church the money is there. There just seems to be little understanding or vision for integral mission, or for anything outside of the Thai context. Seminaries teach courses on evangelism, on using tracts, on giving altar calls. But very little is taught about reaching the whole person through word and action together.

There was one development project in Sivilai that both the community and church got behind. The land behind the church where the cockfighting arena was located came up for sale. We managed to raise money and the church bought it. We then had to decide as a church how to use it. At that time the only preschool in Sivilai was at the temple and could not meet the demand of the community. So Sivilai Samaki Nursery School was built. Nip, who had come with her husband Py to be the pastors of the church and take over from us, was the first headteacher. She and another church member travelled to Bangkok, and spent a couple of days in a CCT church preschool in Klong Toey slum that uses the Montessori method of teaching. Church members rallied around to help with the actual construction and we ended up with a small school with two classrooms, a dining room area, bathrooms, and special sinks for face-washing and tooth-brushing. We already had playground equipment in the church compound, which was well used every day by the village kids. The only thing we had to do was put up a flagpole.

Once everything was ready we had the grand opening ceremony. The mayor came along with various other civil servants and representatives from places like the hospital, the schools and the police. Church leaders came from the presbytery headquarters. The most important and respected guest was Brigadier Somkit, whom we invited to perform the opening ceremony. His wife Tessa was a good friend of ours from the International Church of Bangkok. He had been a senator and was involved in writing one of Thailand's first constitutions, and his home constituency was in Udon, not too far from Sivilai. By the time we opened the nursery school he was retired. It was wonderful for us to see the respect he was shown by all the attending politicians and dignitaries, especially when in his opening speech he talked about his fairly new Christian faith. It was an amazing witness for the church in Sivilai.

Every morning the two to five-year-olds would stand in line and raise the flag, sing the Thai national anthem and then pray. We had no problem recruiting students, particularly amongst the professional families in town; parents thought their children might get a good start to their education if they went to the foreigners' school! Nip and Jy were enthusiastic teachers and the children had a lot of fun as well as working quite hard! After raising the flag and prayers came energetic aerobics. As well as playing and learning numbers and letters, they did a lot of singing with actions and imaginative play. In true Montessori form, during free play each child put down a square piece of cloth on the floor, went and chose their toy or activity from the shelf, played on his or her own area, and then put it away on the shelf again. It was very, *very* un-Thai, but it worked really well.

Four-year-old Rachel loved it all apart from one aspect. Every afternoon, after lunch, all the children got out their mats and pillows and willingly lay down and slept for an hour, sometimes two. Not Rachel. She refused and actually we did not want her to sleep, because whenever she slept in the daytime she was up all night. So Rachel would come home in the afternoon and do British nursery home-schooling with Mum-turned-teacher.

CHAPTER ELEVEN

Learning Life's Lessons

Tip was about twelve years old when we got to know her. She came along to church and took part in the youth events. She was the only person in her family interested in Christianity, and when she was fourteen Mike baptised her. It was clear she was bright and desperately wanted to go to university to study nursing. However, at that time Sivilai secondary school had never had anyone successfully get into university. We visited Tip in her village and got to know her dad and stepmother. They were very poor.

Tip's father had come from Laos. He was an educated man who had been a respected teacher until he had to flee the country in the 70s when the communists took over. In Thailand, despite the fact that he had fled the communists, people knew he was from Laos and so were suspicious of him, so he ended up a daily labourer and rice farmer, never able to get a teaching job again. He valued education though, and it hurt him that Tip could not get a good one. The final straw for us was when she set fire to her bed trying to do homework by candlelight as they had no electricity.

So we helped to send Tip to a Christian boarding school in Petchaburi, many hours' drive from home. Academically she did well, and after school we supported her through university. When we moved to Bangkok she lived with us and became even closer to us as a family. Three years later Mike conducted her wedding service when she married Kiw. Rachel and Aylie were bridesmaids and I stood in as mother of the bride! Professionally she did very well and became a head nurse in a busy intensive care unit in Bangkok.

However, there have been many times over the years when I have wondered whether we made the right choices for her. It is such a huge responsibility when you have money and power and can make choices for people that change the whole direction of their lives. I do not think Tip would look back and say she regrets what she did and where she is now – married with a gorgeous child – but she certainly suffered. She was very unhappy and homesick away at school and there was little we could do. Was it right to take her away from her family and culture? She finds it hard even to go back and visit now. Was it worth it in order to get a good education and a good job? Many people make sacrifices for education, and I think probably it *is* often worth it. But if we were to do it all over again I would think much more carefully and really weigh up the sacrifice, in a way that I was just too immature and inexperienced to do for Tip. We did what we thought was right and she is happy, but I do sometimes wonder what would have happened in her life if we had not interfered with it.

The Karen, with whom we worked in Sangklaburi, put great value on education and it is often the highest priority for parents in decision-making. The political struggle in Burma and continuous oppression of the Karen since the end of the Second World War has meant that for many it is no longer possible to access education within their own country, particularly for the internally displaced living in the jungle. For those who cross over into Thailand as refugees there is access to schooling in the camps, but the schools are overcrowded and many of the good teachers have been resettled to live in third countries. For the teachers who are left, the pay is minimal and there are few opportunities for further training or motivation. And for Karen migrants who live in Thailand illegally, many are turned away by Thai schools despite the fact that the law states that all children on Thai soil have a right to attend school. Many Karen apply for resettlement in a third country, not for themselves, but in order to give their children a hope for the future. Many resettled Karen adults struggle enormously with the huge adaptation it takes to go from living their whole life in the jungle to moving to a large urban centre in the USA, Australia or Britain. But they consider it worth it for the sake of their children and the educational opportunities that will be open to them that would have been impossible in Burma or a refugee camp in Thailand.

Part of my role with Christ Church Bangkok was as an administrator for the work the church supports on the Burmese border. One of the projects the church supports is a boarding school for Karen migrants, about forty miles north of Mae La – one of the biggest refugee camps, where approximately fifty thousand refugees lived at the time. The school is very close to the river that forms the border with Burma and is on the edge of a small Thai village, next to an army base. The school has close to two hundred secondary school students aged between eleven and twenty-five, half of whom are boarders. Many are older than is usual at school, having been denied the opportunity to attend school when they were younger, usually because they were hiding in the jungle. About a third of the students come from Mae La camp, another third from the village, and a third travel to the school from inside Burma. At least a couple of the children know they have left their families for the whole seven years of secondary education – but they and their families believe it is worth the sacrifice. There is no future for them in Burma.

The kids come with all sorts of emotional baggage and experiences. Some have known no other life than that in a refugee camp. Others have seen family members raped and killed and their villages burnt. Despite the trauma many of the children have experienced, it is an amazingly happy school. There is strong Christian leadership and the school has a very good reputation in the province, both academically and in the kind of mature, reliable youngsters who graduate. The headmistress and the staff are all Karen and the volunteers, who go there to teach English, all come through Christ Church via mission agencies. It really is a remarkable place hidden away in the back of beyond. However, for those who graduate it is still very hard. They do not have Thai citizenship and in theory are not allowed to even consider tertiary education or travel beyond the immediate area around the camp. There is not much hope for the future. These kids come out with better English than many, so some get jobs with local NGOs or faith-based organisations. For others their English language proficiency is good preparation for being resettled to a third country, if they are given the opportunity.

When Rachel was eight years old I found her crying one day in our home in Sangklaburi. When I asked what was wrong, she just kept saying, 'It's not fair.' I assumed she had fought with Aylie or a friend over something, but eventually she was calm enough to explain. She went on to tell me how she knew that not many miles away over the border, in Burma, there were children just like her who were hiding in the jungle without proper shelter from the rain, or food, or even the chance to go to school. She was distraught at the injustice and shouted at me, 'It's not fair and we aren't doing anything about it. They are just like me.'

At only eight years of age Rachel had hit the nail on the head. So often we hear stories about refugees and immediately, without thinking, there is a kind of 'us and them' in our minds. Even though we may be reluctant to admit it, it almost makes what they go through OK, or at least out of our range of responsibility. Either that or we are fearful that in some way those from outside our country will come and take what is rightfully ours. I know there are many Thais who feel that about refugees or migrants from Burma, just as there are many Brits who feel like that about refugees, asylum seekers and migrants in the UK. There is a subconscious fear that somehow we, who have so much, will lose out to these who have suffered so much – or perhaps just that they make us feel guilty for having so much. Rachel, however, had talked about children 'just like me'. In her childlike innocence she had not made that separation. She simply saw children and their parents *just like us* except they had to leave all that was familiar. They had lost all that we assume to be our rights: education, health care, shelter and security. Rachel knew at a heart level that we have a God-given responsibility to reach out, not out of some sort of charity, paternalism or condescension, but because we are the same flesh and blood; we are one family and when refugees are suffering, part of our family is suffering.

When Rachel was fourteen she spent part of her school holidays in Chiang Mai working as a general dogsbody or gopher for the Free Burma Rangers (FBR). FBR was set up by our good friends Dave and Karen, who train ethnic minority teams from Burma to go back into their country and bring relief and stand alongside their people in their suffering. They take medical teams, teachers, pastors and people trained in recording human rights abuses so that the world hears what is happening. Rachel spent the week running around Chiang Mai shopping and packing supplies, working in the office and babysitting for Dave and Karen's kids. Her goal is to go 'inside' Burma with one of the teams one day. In order to qualify she will need to run up Doi Suthep[28] at night in under three hours. It is tough walking over mountains in Burma so teams have to be fit! She wrote her school final year extended essay on the effects on the camps of re-settlement of refugees to third countries, and as a result has interviewed refugees in Britain, Australia, the USA and Mae La camp itself, as well as children from the school Christ Church supports. Rachel has now graduated from university. She has never lost the passion she had as an eight-year-old to help the internally displaced Karen and refugees.

Aylie too caught the vision and when she was nine had all her classmates make special packs containing toiletries, toys, vitamins, a hat and a personal photo and postcard. These were sent into the jungle for the internally displaced children via FBR teams. When she was eleven she researched the whole situation of the internally displaced for her Year Six exhibition and presented her findings in the form of a passionate speech, taking on the persona of a child hiding in the jungle.

I am a proud mum: proud that my children see beyond their own world and empathise with those in such a different world; proud that my kids care about injustice and want to do something about it; proud that they see the value of the health, security and education that is their experience, and understand that for many it is a distant dream; and proud that they are using the amazing education they have received in order to highlight the plight of the many children in Burma who long to have access to the same rights they enjoy.

Our children have had a very privileged life. They are what are commonly known as third-culture kids, although I think they may actually be fourth or fifth-culture kids. They have their British culture, their American culture, the culture of where they lived latterly (Thai / Bangkok / international / urban), the culture of where we lived in the

---

[28] a mountain in Chiang Mai

countryside (Isaan / rural / Karen / Burmese), the culture of where they have lived in Scotland and the combination that produces the culture that is unique to our family! That could make them very confused, mixed-up kids. I think at times they certainly are confused, but they also have a broad understanding of the world; they have experienced, appreciated and learnt from other people's world views; they know they do not have a monopoly on the 'right' way to do things; they have, like me, walked with people who were suffering; they have seen death; they know how to have fun; they have friends scattered all over the world; they have embraced faith; they know and love Christ. They are passionate kids who are engaged with the world and get driven crazy by what they call 'bubble people', who live lives of comfort, oblivious to the world around them. It was the culture shock Rachel experienced on moving to Bangkok, when faced with peers who laughed about poverty and injustice and worried more about fashion and parties, that upset her the most. There were some who understood her though, and her best friends over the years have been Israeli, Danish, American, Indian, Korean, Polish and Thai.

Rachel's first language for a while was Isaan, followed by Thai and then English. Much of her English came from Sesame Street videos! But language is a strange thing. Children pick it up so easily but they also lose it when they are young. The almost two years we spent in the UK when Rachel was five meant that on our return to Thailand she was frustrated for six months, unable to communicate with the people around her. Her frustration was the main reason we sent her to Thai school for a term, as well as giving her the opportunity to make friends.

Aylie's experience of Thailand when she was small was Sangklaburi. She did not go to school but had a Karen nanny. We knew she could speak quite good Karen and English. Every Sunday she would pop next door to Doe's house for tiny little fried fish. One day, Doe brought her home and mentioned in passing how much Aylie had enjoyed chatting to all the Burmese people who had been visiting. I said, 'Oh, so they speak Karen,' and Doe laughed. 'No,' she replied, 'Aylie speaks pretty good Burmese!' We had no idea. Once we were in Bangkok the Karen and Burmese were forgotten but both kids speak fluent Thai, albeit teenage vocabulary; and pretty good Spanish, a subject at school; as well as English, mixed with American!

139

Despite functioning in different languages, Aylie has always had an incredibly rich vocabulary, which is particularly apparent in her extraordinarily imaginative writing. Rachel also loves to write and many people enjoyed reading her newsletter *The Minnows* over the years. When we moved to Bangkok and got together with a friend who had never actually met the children, she asked Rachel where her big sister was. She assumed the author of Minnows was at least sixteen, never imagining it was the eleven-year-old she was talking to!

First words were interesting for both the girls as well. Rachel's first word, as I mentioned earlier, was 'baebae' – the sounds the goats made. Her other favourite was *'by'*, which means 'let's go' in Thai and which she said constantly. Aylie was learning to talk in the months after we moved to Sangklaburi and her first word was *'fymy'* or 'fire' – as we listened to the forest fires getting closer and closer; bamboo makes a spectacularly frightening noise when it burns, as the hollow stalks fill with hot air and explode.

CHAPTER TWELVE

The Forces of Nature

Forest fires are very frightening. We have never experienced anything like the fires in Australia or California. But burning bamboo in the jungle is terrifying. In rural Thailand in January, when there has been no rain for a few months, some people try to burn off the overgrown undergrowth along the roads, and fires often spread out of control. On one occasion, Mike and all the other men in the community in Sangklaburi had to dig trenches to try to prevent a fire from encroaching on the church compound, while I hurriedly packed all our valuables and documents into the car. When all the houses are made of wood it is particularly scary. Amazingly, I never heard of the forest fires actually destroying houses or people being hurt, but they came close on a number of occasions.

There was one fire in Sangklaburi that destroyed homes and badly injured at least one person. This was not a forest fire though. It was the result of someone turning on the ignition of their car while filling up with fuel from one of the basic petrol stations like the one we ran. The petrol station has a huge fifty-five-gallon barrel of fuel which is hand-pumped into the vehicle, so when a fire is ignited it is like a massive bomb – or two or three depending on how many tanks there are. Health and safety laws may exist but are rarely enforced or even acknowledged, and somehow one becomes accepting of the fact, as if it's the norm – until a tragedy like this happens.

Along with the rest of the world, we watched in horror as the tsunami of Boxing Day 2004 caused unbelievable destruction across large parts of the world, including southern Thailand. It was so awful feeling unable to help, so I was pleased when someone from the CCT Bangkok Christian Hospital called me and asked if I would be willing to go on a team to give medical aid. Sadly, they took forever to get their act together and by the time we got there on 30th December we found little but dead bodies. We were able to help a couple of small communities, who were still sheltering in the hills, but I felt completely helpless as we and many other medical teams from around the world sat around the small hospitals, surrounded by bodies, unable to do anything useful. What they needed were forensic experts to identify the dead. All the injured had already been airlifted out. Later there were many needs as communities struggled with their loss and tried to rebuild. But in those first few days it was like something out of a horror film.

Flooding has always been an issue in Thailand but 2011 saw floods on a scale that had not been seen for fifty years. In December 2011 I received a Christmas letter from a friend, a retired missionary who had worked for many years in Thailand. She reminisced about the floods fifty years earlier which she remembered well, as they had coincided with her daughter's birth. She wrote:

> We were in the town of Inburi in the province of Singburi. To get to the hospital we had to use three boats, changing in Singburi and then in Manorom to a small boat, which took us into the hospital compound, which had about 9 feet of water in it.

Incredible. Or so it would have seemed if I had read this a year earlier, probably thinking, 'Thank goodness that will never happen again in Thailand – a developed country.' And yet in 2011 the floods were, in some places, including Manorom, as bad if not worse than in 1961. A third of the country was under up to three metres of water, hundreds of thousands of people lost their homes and jobs, over six hundred lost their lives, thousands were sick or injured, and there was little hope for many.

At a national level the economic cost of the flooding was huge, but at a local level it was absolutely devastating for many, many people. The poor, the weak and the vulnerable are the ones who suffered the long-term effects the most. They did not have insurance policies or second homes. They did not have savings or alternative ways of making ends meet. We, like others, did our bit as far as preparing food and taking it by boat to stranded people and packaging up relief supplies at one of the national relief centres. We felt guilty at how stressed we became with the constant not knowing if the water would come or not – guilty because we stayed dry when others went under and guilty because the stress it caused seemed out of proportion when you compare it to that endured by those who lost so much.

The Office of Child Protection, where Mike worked, realised early on that children suffer from these floods more than anyone else. They produced a wonderful workbook for kids based on the story of Noah, to help them work through their trauma and sadness, sense of loss and hopelessness. It helped the children look at their experiences, express their emotions and then move on in hope. It was practical, colourful and fun. Just as Noah sent out the dove, who came back eventually with an olive branch, a sign of hope to an end to the suffering, so the OCP longs to see children telling their own stories of suffering and so coming eventually to a place of hope.

Water is a strong force and destructive even on a small scale. Our front door in Sivilai was actually a double door opening in the middle, in order to be wide enough to get the tractor in. The downstairs of our house doubled up as a garage for Mike's motorbike and the tractor. Until you do it, it is difficult to imagine how hard it is to build a door frame and doors to exactly the correct measurements and successfully hang the doors! It was a learning experience for Mike although he might describe it more as a trial. But he did it and he was so proud of this achievement he painted the doors bright red. They were perfect – or so we thought, until the night of the big storm!

I do not think I ever slept soundly in Sivilai. There was always some noise to wake you, whether a cockerel, or radio, or gangs of dogs. Personally I found the sound of rain on the tin roof[29] incredibly soothing. It rarely woke me up. If it did, or if there was wind as well, I would make a quick check to ensure windows were shut and sun-blinds down, to prevent the rain flooding our big open landing; then I would

---

[29] We had no ceiling.

enjoy the sound of the rain and fall straight back to sleep. One poor friend who visited in the rainy season never got used to the incredibly loud noise it makes and I do not think she slept for three weeks.

On the night of the 'big storm' we had another friend staying – Andy, the friend whose mosquito net had filled with bugs when he was reading in bed.[30] It rained hard during the night and the wind was blowing. Andy could not sleep and so went downstairs to get a drink and that was when he screamed and woke us all up. He had not turned the lights on and when he stepped down from the second stair he found himself literally in deep water. There was a foot of water through the house. We were perplexed when he called up to tell us. Where was it coming from? The upstairs was fine. We soon found out, as with the lights on we saw Niagara Falls pouring down the inside of our beautifully fitted double front doors!

---

[30] See page 43.

CHAPTER THIRTEEN

Moving Out of Comfort Zones

When we got married, good friends who know us well gave us a visitors' book. In the front was a quotation from Edith Schaeffer's 'What is a Family?'[31] It read, 'A family is a door that has hinges and a lock.' I think our friends were trying to remind us that it is good and right to be hospitable but there are times to shut the door. It is a lesson we have tried to learn.

During our first year living in Bangkok we had little official support from our mission or anyone on the ground, but that also meant little supervision. I think these days mission agencies usually recommend that people try not to have visitors or travel during their first year, in order to allow time to adapt to the new place and to learn the language undistracted. We had no one keeping an eye on us or advising us about things like that and at the end of the year we worked out that we'd had just six weeks out of fifty-two without visitors staying in our home. Each one was God-appointed and when we looked back we could see either how staying with us had blessed them in some specific way, or that God had used them to bless or teach us. I am not sure how we ever actually learned any Thai though!

As part of his Masters in Theology, Culture and Development in Edinburgh, Mike wrote a dissertation on pilgrimage. He was looking particularly at short-term mission trips with the idea of them being pilgrimage to the poor. One of the things he talked about was liminality

---

[31] *What is a Family?* Edith Schaeffer; Baker Publishing Group (1975)

– going to the limits, pushing the boundaries. He looked at the need for people to be pushed beyond their normal limits or comfort zones, in fact even the need for a certain level of suffering as part of the trip, if they are really to grow and be changed through the experience.

I am not sure that Mum and Dad saw the benefits of suffering on their first trip to Thailand. We were young and enthusiastic, and committed to a simple lifestyle. Unfortunately, we were rather blinkered, and did not realise that not everyone was enthralled by long, sweaty city bus rides, dusty Isaan roads, local fly-covered markets, third-class trains, streetside meals and no air-conditioning. They endured a lot on that visit. We eventually came to our senses and so for their last meal took them to a fancy hotel where Mum indulged in lobster. Sadly, it was spoiled and she spent the whole flight home throwing up. So much for the benefits of indulging in a bit of luxury!

Sometimes a visitor's journey to the limits has also caused us some stress too. Glenn was a regular visitor when we lived in Bangkok. He and I nursed together, came to Thailand at the same time, and then went to Bible college together. He ended up in Cambodia and would often come and visit on his travels in the region. On one such visit the three of us decided to go to spend a weekend in Kanchanaburi, on raft-house-type accommodation near the Bridge over the River Kwai. It was very pretty and idyllic – predating the loud disco boats that blast their way up and down the river on weekends these days. In the evening we went out to dinner at a typical riverside restaurant. We got chatting to a group of guys on the next table – despite us not having much Thai and Glenn having none. When we had finished eating, Mike and I were ready to go but Glenn was having fun so decided to stay, promising not to come in too late as we were all in the same raft house.

Well, very early on in our marriage we got a taste of what parents of teenagers go through! By midnight I was already trying to work out where the local police station was, by 2 am I was trying to go through my address book in my mind to see if we had Glenn's boss's number in Cambodia, and by 4 am I was mentally dredging the river! Glenn did not come home all night. Talk about panic stations! Eventually at about 8 am he staggered into the raft house.

He had experienced an interesting and long night. When the meal finished his new friends had invited him to visit their home. (What do we teach our kids about getting into cars with strangers?) He reckoned it was for a quick coffee somewhere in town, so he jumped in the car. But they did not go home. They went where many Thai men go to round off an evening out: a brothel. It was in the middle of nowhere and they were quite offended when Glenn said he would rather stay in the car – but he did. Once they came out again, they headed for home, which turned out to be far out of the city. Once there, they had no plans to come back again until morning. So Glenn certainly stepped out of his comfort zone – and dragged us with him.

Stepping out of one's comfort zone comes in many forms. It could just be the heat and constant sweating, squat toilets or unfamiliar food. It could be being challenged by 'strange' cultural norms, whether acceptable or unacceptable. For many it is deeper than that. It is being confronted by things we do not understand: by poverty and injustice; by powerlessness and vulnerability; and sometimes just by different values or ways of thinking.

Wanting to be able to fix things and solve all the problems and pain can be exhausting and very frustrating for anyone, especially without language or an understanding of culture. Throwing money at people is often the knee-jerk reaction and usually inappropriate. Watching, listening and learning from those who can interpret the situation will help. It has been a real privilege for us to host people from Thailand and all over the world as part of their own journeys – some as tourists, some as short-term volunteers and some for longer. Some came for one-off visits, and others repeat appearances. Our visitors' books are wonderful records for looking back and I love re-reading them and remembering the stories behind each entry. My prayer for visitors and short-term workers who came to us in Thailand was that they would return home with an expanded world view; with a deeper understanding that other ways of thinking and doing things are different, not wrong; with an ability to critique their own culture; with an empathy for some of the struggles that the poor and the powerless go through; with a heightened passion for justice and a desire to get involved in order to pursue it; with a longing to see people being transformed through encounter with Jesus; and with itchy feet to get out into the world again and learn more!

CHAPTER FOURTEEN

Right, Wrong and the Uncharted Waters in Between

Beggars are a normal sight on the streets of Bangkok. Normal to those who live there and walk past them every day. Normal, often to the point of invisibility. Shocking perhaps to those who come from the affluent West and are not used to having poverty and desperation thrown in their face – but even then eyes glaze over very fast and beggars become invisible a day or two after arrival.

When I did orientation for new people coming to Thailand, one of the questions they always asked was whether they should give money to beggars. If you ask many foreigners what they 'do about beggars', the majority will tell you that you should not give to them. Some justify this stance by explaining that most beggars are put out on the streets by gangs who take all the money anyway, and so by giving you perpetuate the cycle. Others will say that people should earn their money and not beg for it. Some say, if you give a beggar money for food he will probably spend it on drugs or alcohol. Among the Christian community there is sometimes the feeling that if Buddhists see us giving to beggars they will assume that our motive is to make merit. Some just feel that the beggars are not their problem. Dirty, smelly or deformed beggars may physically repulse, causing people to give them a wide berth.

A few years ago I found myself horrified by my own reaction to a beggar. She had no face, just folds of skin that hung down to her chest with small openings for mouth and nose, and no eyes. She looked literally repulsive. I was reminded one day, as I almost walked past her as usual, of what Jesus says about when we touch people like her we are touching Him, and so I sat down on the pavement and talked to her. She told me her story. She had been born with her deformity in a small village in Isaan. Amazingly, she was not rejected by her family, as is common in Thailand, and now at the age of forty she lived with her sister in a rented room in Bangkok. Her sister had a job, and begging was this woman's way of contributing to the household.

We chatted two or three times after that and my whole attitude to her changed. By hearing her story, she became a fellow human being to me rather than the monster that she clearly seemed to be for the majority who walked passed her each day. She was not my problem – but I was still able to give her dignity by acknowledging her existence. And yet so often I, and probably you, just walk on by.

It is often true that in many cases where children or the disabled are begging, they will not receive the money they collect; and by giving we perpetuate this abominable exploitation of the vulnerable. But, if that child gets to the end of the day with no money to hand over, she or he will probably be beaten. Giving a few coins might stave off that beating.

When we lived upcountry and came on short trips to Bangkok my children would never accept beggars, especially other children, as normal. I used to have to carry a backpack full of cartons of milk on my back, ready to give them to any young child sitting on the pavement with the obligatory empty McDonalds paper cup and look of desperation, resignation and vulnerability.

A friend in Bangkok wrote an article about begging which I always showed to new people when they first arrived as it gives yet another perspective. This is some of what she wrote:

I was walking along a busy road in the middle of Bangkok, on my way to pick up the kids from school. As usually happens, I was struggling to decide whether to give to the beggar I could see ahead or not. Sometimes I do, sometimes I don't. I thought, 'Oh well, err on the side of generosity,' and I had some spare change handy. I went up to the man, who obviously was very deformed by leprosy, and leant over to put a few coins in his cup. He then put his fingerless hand over the cup and shook his head indicating he didn't want the money. Now this is something that had never happened before. I looked at him questioningly and he did the same thing again. I said in Thai, 'Are you sure you don't want it?' and he replied, 'It's Rachael, isn't it? From Chiang Mai?' All of a sudden I realised who he was. It was Manut (not his real name). I'd thought his face was familiar but had assumed it was because of the characteristic sunken nose and thick skin instead of eyebrows that often accompanies severe cases of leprosy. I'd become used to this appearance years ago when working at McKean, a leprosy rehabilitation centre in Chiang Mai.

I squatted on the pavement next to him and we chatted animatedly as long lost friends. We reminisced about the people we remembered from McKean over ten years earlier and he told me of those he was still in touch with. He said, 'I've still got that photo pinned up at home of the time you and big brother Scott took us all out on a picnic to the gardens at the Hot Springs.' We've got photos of that picnic at home as well. It was a great day. We squeezed at least 25 young people – all with disabilities of one sort or another, mostly leprosy – into two small vans, together with wheelchairs, crutches, food and guitars. It was a rare opportunity for them to get out of the hospital and go somewhere special. I remember one photo in our album of Manut as a young man, already terribly disfigured by leprosy, on a swing, surrounded by friends, smiling away.

Manut looked down and said how he didn't want to have to be begging like this. He looked somewhat embarrassed. Obviously when someone spends over a year in a leprosy rehabilitation centre the hope isn't that they'll end up begging on the street. Then suddenly he lifted up his head, smiled and said, 'But all I need is another 20,000 baht and I'll have enough to pay off my house!' I listened attentively as he excitedly told me about the home he lives in on the edge of Bangkok with his parents and his wife who works as a

150

cleaner and how he is a member of a church there. It was at about his point that I realised I was quite late to get my kids and I'd have to say goodbye. We said how great it was to see each other and I wished him God's blessing in his life, trying desperately by my smile and affection to send the message that I understood how this for him was a legitimate way to contribute to the needs of his family. With completely dysfunctional hands and the obvious signs of leprosy on his face, his options for employment were almost non-existent in a city like Bangkok.

As I got up to leave, I became aware of what an interesting spectacle we had been for the passers-by, many of whom were taking a second look over their shoulder. It's not every day you see a foreign woman squatting on a busy pavement, laughing and chatting in Thai with a beggar, oblivious to everyone else. I was so full of joy at this chance encounter and laughed to myself as I walked to the school. I thought about my friend trying to pay his mortgage like most of us do. He was no longer the faceless beggar whose life was totally removed and worlds away from mine. His dignity was expressed in his struggle to support his family the best he could. And what was significant in our relationship was not charity or pity but friendship, a common experience, a genuine joy in acknowledging the humanity of another person.

So now you're probably saying, these beggars obviously can't be that badly off if they're buying houses. It kind of made the response of giving all beggars food instead of money seem a bit out of touch. Plates of cold rice or cartons of milk don't pay the mortgage. I don't think I've solved my dilemma about whether to give money to beggars or not. But from now on I'll certainly try to look them in the eye and remember that they are people just like you and me who have individual stories, hopes, dreams and lives just as real and significant as our own.

Rachael Litchfield

In the end I told new people that there is no answer as to whether or not to give to beggars. I suggested that it is worth having coins or small denomination notes in one's pocket, and to just be open to God's prompting. Like Rachael, I also told people that one thing we can give people is dignity, recognising them as visible fellow human beings, making eye contact, smiling and saying hallo, or even sitting on the pavement for a chat.

When living and working cross-culturally, it is an everyday occurrence to ask, 'When is it right to do what is not right, and what is right anyway?' We think we know the difference between right and wrong, between truth and falsehood. We think we know what truth is. And yet when we look at situations through the lenses of someone else's world view they may have a different perspective on what is right and wrong, on what truth is. I recently heard a missionary say that she copes with this dilemma by always 'running everything through the filter of the Bible'. I then challenged her by saying, 'But the way you read and understand the Bible may not be the same as another, particularly someone from a different culture.' We, from our Western world view, do not have the monopoly on hermeneutics. In fact, we are probably farther from understanding the culture and context of the Bible than someone from the East.

One example of different interpretations of what is important is the concept of the value of truth. In the West we understand that truthfulness is very important for Christians, and that it is a godly attribute. We would probably say it is one of the most important Biblical values. In Thailand, although no one would dispute the importance of truth, the way people live and relate shows that actually preservation of relationship is more important than truth. Thai Christians will argue that this too is a Biblical value. So who is right? This high value placed on preserving relationship revolves around face; preserving face or losing face. If by our actions we cause someone to lose face, we spoil a relationship. So for example, if someone offers you something you really do not want it is better to lie and say, 'Yes, please,' and take it, than to reject it, causing loss of face and spoilt relationship. If you ask an employee directly if they will do something for you, they will always say yes, because to say no would cause you to lose face, even if actually they have no intention of doing it. The disappointment felt will come later when you are not together and so no face will be lost and the negative effect on relationship will be less, they believe. These are very superficial examples, but this way of thinking runs deep into every area of life.

Ethical dilemmas abound when living in Thailand. Corruption exists at many levels. What do you do about the traffic cop who would rather do you a favour when he stops you and take cash for his pocket, than write an official ticket which costs more in money but also in your time as you have to pay it at the police station? Do you take the easy route? It happens a lot at the end of the month when these guys are running out of money because they are paid so badly. Surely it is the simplest solution and keeps everyone happy. But should we not be taking a stand and doing what we know is right – even if it is not the easiest way? As Christians, are we not called to render to Caesar what is Caesar's? Surely that means abiding by the law at all times unless it contradicts what we believe, and not just when it is convenient.

But what about the times when there really does not seem to be a legal option? When we moved to Sivilai we needed somehow to build a house. We lived with a family initially, but the congregation wanted a manse/vicarage for us on the church property that could be an extension of the church building for Sunday school, lunches, and other meetings, as well as our home. They, and we, wanted a house in the traditional style of the village – built out of wood, standing on concrete pillars. But where were we to get the wood? There seemed to be two options: to cut it illegally, or to buy illegally cut wood from the corrupt police. Neither option was one we felt we could go ahead with. We had to be careful because it really seemed that these were the only possibilities and every one of our church members would have to have gone down one line or the other when they built their own houses. Brick was too expensive. There seemed no point in rubbing in the fact that they had done something wrong. In the end they justified us not wanting to go down either route by saying that this was God's house they were building and so should be 'pure'. But we still had no way of getting wood.

After a couple of months of wondering, praying and discussing, God provided the answer. The mother of a church member, Don, died and the family sold us her house. It was on the other side of the village so we moved it – literally took it down piece by piece and carried it on wheelbarrows and carts to the church, where it was reassembled. Church members built the new manse with Don as foreman. We had a traditional wooden upstairs, but also a brick downstairs providing a bathroom, kitchen, office and place to park the tractor. We stayed within the law so the house was 'pure'.

Big business is rife with practices that some would find unacceptable. Nepotism, plagiarism, discrimination and 'taking a cut' from a budget for work are the norm. I suspect they are often the norm in the UK too but perhaps less obvious. You can't advertise a job for someone of a certain gender, age or race in the UK, whereas this is completely accepted in Thailand, if they advertise at all. Most jobs are given to relatives or friends of the boss, whether the job is leading political parties or working as a labourer. When Mike was a member of Sathorn Church, in Bangkok, he met many wealthy businessmen who were keen to run their businesses under Kingdom values. They invited Mike to teach a series of sessions on Christian business ethics. It was exciting to see their enthusiasm to be different and stand out in the business world, even if it meant making less money.

The business of piracy is a major source of income for Thailand. And I am not talking about piracy at sea! When we first moved to Bangkok our landlady was the head of a music piracy company that in those days could turn out something like thirty thousand cassette tapes an hour. In fact, the house she gave us to live in had previously been a pirate tape factory! She was, rumour had it, one of the seven most wanted women in the USA.

You can buy any kind of designer label that you want to on the streets and in the markets. DVDs and CDs are everywhere for as little as two pounds. It is difficult to find a legal way to get BBC iPlayer outside the UK, but it is easy to download whole series of TV off the Internet, not to mention movies. Using software that is banned in the UK is easy, and it makes up for not being able to watch the TV we would get at home. But is that good enough justification, or as Christians, should we say no? I know many who do and I admire them for it. I confess that we have not. We have bought the movies and downloaded the TV. Interestingly though, as we talked about moving back to the UK we were of one mind that even though we had already committed a crime by buying them, it would be a worse crime to take them to the UK where somehow they seemed more illegal. So our DVDs, CDs and downloads stayed behind!

I had not really thought about clothes though. We have never been into looking specifically to buy clothes with the right labels on them, but we may have bought designer labelled clothes inadvertently. I had to look through our wardrobes and see if we had any fake designer attire. If we did, would we take it or leave it? When Mike and I worked in the immigration detention centre we had contact with a big international law firm. One day they called us and asked if we could use a couple of thousand good quality shirts for the prisoners. We leapt at the offer but there was an interesting catch. These clothes were in the law firm's possession as the result of a crackdown on piracy. They were all fake Lacoste shirts and we could only have them if we first cut off every label and cut out every crocodile motif! It took days of sitting in the law firm's air conditioned offices, and the shirts ended up with a small croc shaped hole on the left hand side – but it was worth every minute, and makes me smile every time I see a Lacoste shirt! I did not find any fake designer clothes when I sorted out what to pack. But if I had, all I would have needed was a pair of scissors with which to remove any logos or labels, even if it meant going back with holey clothes.

Living on the border of Burma, most of the people we lived and worked with did not have Thai citizenship. Many had lived in Thailand for two or three generations. Their children were born there. By Thai law they should have been afforded citizenship and the rights that go with it. In reality this did not often happen. They described themselves as people who had fallen down the crack between two civilisations. There are official channels whereby people can apply for citizenship and, if they meet the criteria, can in theory get Thai papers. But progress is often hampered by corrupt officials wanting 'back-handers' in order to sign documents or agree to process papers. Sometimes money changes hands and still nothing happens.

Mike was involved with a church project to try to help people to get the citizenship they were entitled to. The project involved hours of form-filling and paperwork and as a result some did end up getting citizenship, but many are still waiting. Those without citizenship are more vulnerable and this often leads to them being exploited and oppressed; people who on paper do not even exist are easy prey for trafficking and abuse. When this happens, the impact of corruption is more sinister. The use and abuse of money in order to buy one's way out of justice is sadly common, especially if the victim is poor and voiceless. We have seen this particularly in the area of child abuse.

CHAPTER FIFTEEN

Let the Little Ones Come to Me

There are very few placed in the Bible where Jesus actually advocates or models violence. The most well-known is when he upturns the tables of the money changers and market stalls in the temple during holy week. It was shocking. We talk about his anger being righteous and appropriate as he challenged the defilement of the temple. Yet I think Jesus is even stronger in his indignant anger with, and threats towards, those who defile children. Mark 9:42 says, 'If one of these little children believes in me, and someone causes that child to sin, it would be better for that person to have a large stone tied around his neck and be drowned in the sea.' It is strong stuff. It is an example of Jesus' heart for the vulnerable, the abused, the oppressed, the young in faith. He called children to sit with him and said clearly that they were to be valued. We see God's heart for children in Jesus.

At about the time we were leaving Sangklaburi in 2005, we became very aware that children in border areas are particularly at risk of abuse. When I mention the risks of border living, people often think first of trafficking. Yes, human trafficking is a major problem, but abuse within the hundreds of orphanages, hostels, dormitories and other kinds of homes where children are brought together is far more of a problem, and sadly the Christians are not immune. In fact, when a friend was talking to the head social worker of one province where there are a particularly large number of institutions looking after children, she said, 'Buddhists run them badly, Muslims train insurgents, and Christians abuse.' It is shocking. It is not usually intentional. But

157

people (often foreigners) with big hearts, but also a lack of understanding of both culture and child protection issues, set up institutions that do not have safeguards in place.

The small church where we worshipped in Sangklaburi really valued the importance of education, as most Karen do. They had discovered a community of illegal Karen migrants living in the forest outside of town – the people who described themselves as having 'fallen down the crack between two civilisations'. They lived in abject poverty and had no way of accessing education or health care. The church opened a small school. There were two teachers – Thai and Karen – who received tiny salaries but gave everything they could to make the school a success. The church rented a basic building with a tin roof and mud floor, bamboo benches and tables. The children did not receive the quality of education my kids received in Bangkok, but they were being taught.

One day a British backpacker was passing through and stumbled across the school. Within about two weeks, and just as we were leaving, he had convinced five families that he could do a better job at raising their kids, with promises of high-level education and possibly citizenship. He basically told them that if they really loved their children, they would hand them over to him to raise. There were no social workers to intervene on behalf of voiceless people. He had a good heart but no understanding of children's needs e.g. being with family or community, and certainly no understanding of Karen culture. Eight years later he had over a hundred children in his care. He was able to establish a foundation in the UK, which attracts money for the 'poor Karen orphans', very few of whom are orphans at all,[32] with no obvious understanding by charity commissioners of the situation on the ground. For a long time, he was not able to register as a foundation in Thailand as he did not meet the requirements. Local people, who had the children's interests at heart, expressed concern that these kids no longer knew their own culture. There seemed to be little discipline or structure and the children had a reputation in the town for 'running wild'.

This was one example of many along Thailand's borders of people, probably with the best intentions, taking children from their families

---

[32] It is estimated that under three per cent of children in orphanages or children's homes are actual orphans.

and culture and, just by their situation of living all together, putting them at huge risk of abuse. Even where children are genuinely in need of care, many of the caregivers are totally unaware of the need for active child protection. Lack of awareness leads to an increased possibility of abuse taking place.

The Office of Child Protection of the CCT initially grew out of our desire to see something being done to help keep children like the ones we saw in Sangklaburi safe. The manager of the team was a young man who caught the vision for child protection when he was doing a Masters in Theology and did Mike's ethics course, studying Amos and his critique of culture. He had previously been an art teacher, and then a youth pastor, and he caught the vision of God's heart for children. He and the rest of the team worked to raise awareness in children's institutions about child protection, taught kids how to protect themselves, helped organisations develop child-safe policies – and, more importantly, implement and evaluate them.

Not only did the project staff team work with institutions and adults to establish child-safe places, they also worked with the children themselves. The team developed a great education programme called 3-3-5, which aimed to teach children how to keep themselves safe and what to do if they or a friend felt threatened or were actually abused. The whole programme revolved around games and activities, whilst at the same time equipping them with the skills they needed to stay safe.

As they did all of these activities, the Office of Child Protection (OCP) team inevitably came across tragic cases of abuse. Sadly, in many of the cases they dealt with, there was little satisfaction of a just resolution. More often than not perpetrators were the rich and powerful, preying on the weak and vulnerable and, in a society where money can still buy anything, that meant they regularly escaped justice. One example was of a man who raped an eight-year-old migrant child so violently she almost bled to death. As a migrant child she was voiceless and powerless, and the man is still free having given the police chief a gift of 100,000 baht. Everyone knows who he is and what he did. He still lives in his village, whilst the child and her family have now disappeared. The victims became the guilty party if they had no money or voice.

Sadly, other perpetrators were pastors in the church. Sometimes they got away with it because they had money. More often the church covered up what had happened in order to save the institution's reputation, with no thought for the victims who were left damaged and discarded by the organisation purporting to demonstrate God's love.

The team were able to help one little girl escape from the cycle of abuse. Amy was three years old. When some missionaries working in the area found her she had two broken legs and a broken arm. She was living with an uncle whilst her mum had gone to Bangkok to work. Over weeks they had witnessed the signs of physical abuse. When he finally hurt her so badly her bones were broken they took her to the hospital. There were no social services to step in, but they persuaded the family that they would not be able to manage to care for the plaster casts and nursing she would need and they took her to their own home. Eventually they were not able to continue to care for Amy and were also afraid because the perpetrator knew where they lived. So Amy moved in with Doe and the other kids she cares for. She was loved and cherished and really flourished. The OCP team knew she would not be safe there forever and that her presence was also putting Doe and the other children at risk. So when her limbs healed, with many tears in Doe's home, they moved her to a home in Kanchanaburi. Amazingly, soon after that her real mum came forward. She had known nothing of the terrible treatment her daughter had been the victim of and she was devastated. As far as we know they have been reunited, and although her mum is desperately poor, at least she loves her and will not beat her.

So much domestic violence against children and women happens in Thailand behind closed doors. Government child protection officers are beginning to realise it should be stopped, but they are fearfully understaffed and only scratch the surface of the problem which runs very deep. They are happy to work together with the Office of Child Protection team as they try to protect the most vulnerable.

Abandoned children are very rare in Karen culture. Usually there is someone who will take in a child within an extended family or community. However, there are occasions when children are really on their own, and intervention is required.

Doe and I met Seng in about 2004. She had three boys, Ben (eleven), Tom (six) and Nate (six). We got to know her because Tom has cerebral palsy and was being cared for by Candlelight, a church agency, with which I was involved and which looked after the disabled in the community. The Candlelight staff noticed that Seng seemed to be sicker every time they visited. So we took her to the hospital where she was found to have TB and AIDS. She was very ill.

We visited them at home regularly and eventually they moved into the TB accommodation at the hospital. Even then Ben looked after the younger boys. He was such a strong child. But one day when I went to the funeral of one of the other patients, Ben suddenly broke down on the way back and sobbed his heart out in the back of the truck. I climbed back and held him whilst he cried, and am so glad I did.

A week later his mum went home to their village to die. Her dearest wish was that Ben would become a novice monk to make merit for her. Of course he fulfilled her wish and so for the last week of her life he sat beside her in his saffron robes, unable to touch her or be held by her or hold her.[33] He was so desperately alone. We were in the house with them when she died and I saw the look of desperation on this child's face as he shouldered the death of his mother in isolation. Doe and I sprang into action and I literally swept the six children[34] there into the car and drove to the hospital to buy formalin to inject into her body.[35] It relieved the tension for the kids as the excitement of being in a car masked the agony of watching Seng die.

On the third day of the funeral she was cremated. We walked in a long procession to the temple, which was deep in the forest. I sat with the children as the monks chanted and her coffin was placed in the oven. The little ones were both crying, Tom on Doe's lap and Nate on

---

[33] Buddhist monks are defiled if they touch a woman.

[34] Seng's three, plus her younger seven-year-old brother and two nephews aged four and one

[35] After death a body may be in the home for three or four days before cremation. With no refrigeration and hot weather, it is necessary to 'preserve' bodies by injecting formaldehyde or formalin soon after death. There were no undertakers to perform these services in rural areas.

mine. However, suddenly Nate stopped crying and looked up to the very high chimney, where smoke from the oven was coming out. He smiled and turned to me and said, 'Oh, everything will be OK now. There is a window so Mummy has gone to be with Jesus.' At that point I started to cry. We don't remember talking to him about Jesus although we had prayed with his mum. She remained a Buddhist as far as we know, although more and more I believe none of us has any clue of what happens to people spiritually when they are actually dying. But when they lived at the Christian Hospital they would have heard the gospel – and it gave Nate hope, as a six-year-old grieving child.

The boys moved home with their grandmother. She was already caring for her own seven-year-old and the two other little grandchildren whose mother had also died. Doe and I visited regularly and very soon they asked if they could call Doe 'Mum'. After a while Doe realised she never saw Granny. She was spending more and more time, often two weeks at a time, foraging in the forest. Ben was responsible for five younger children and he was only eleven years old. He had dropped out of school. Tom could not even sit up and needed everything done for him. To add to everything else, Nate was diagnosed HIV positive. So after much discussion with family and the village head man, Doe officially took the children in and started the family home. The building that had previously housed the co-op store and petrol station[36] was empty and she got permission from the presbytery to take it over. At the same time as taking in the three boys, she also adopted Pupa – a six-year-old girl with cerebral palsy, abandoned early on by her parents, who Candlelight had placed in five successive foster homes, each of which had given her up. She needed stability and love.

Stability and love is what the family home provided. After about a year Tom went to McKean rehabilitation hospital in Chiang Mai with a caregiver for a few months. We visited him there and he was so thrilled to see us. Intensive physio and provision of appropriate equipment meant that by the time he came back, he could sit in a chair and could feed himself. He later learnt to pull himself into a sitting position and move around, by rolling. Over the coming years he was able to attend school for a period, with a caregiver, and became a cheerful, stimulated

---

[36] This was a failed project in the sense that it collapsed when we left.

young man. Although Nate is very small for his age, he did well on ARV medication, which he took faithfully at exactly the right time each day.

In December 2009, Doe got a call from a nurse at Sangklaburi hospital asking her to come and talk to a family. When she arrived she found a Lao couple, refugees who had come through Burma to Thailand, with a sick boy, who looked about seven years old. He had just been diagnosed as having AIDS. The couple then explained that they weren't actually his parents but found him wandering in the market when he was about four. They decided to take him in and care for him out of the goodness of their hearts, because they wanted a son. No one thought of going to authorities, no one asked where this child they were suddenly raising had appeared from. They told Doe and the hospital staff that they now had a biological son of their own, so they did not want him anymore because of his AIDS diagnosis. Doe spent a month visiting, trying to encourage them and support them in caring for him, but one day, despite all her efforts, she came home and found him on her doorstep. They refused to take him back. It's hard to imagine rejection like that at such a young age. So Bill joined the family home, where he was welcomed by Tom, Nate, Ben and Pupa.

It turned out that Bill was actually ten years old. His birth mum had AIDS and was mentally ill. For the previous fourteen years she had lived in a safe house for migrants who have mental illness, in Huay Malai – the village where the Christian hospital, school and Candlelight were located. She was not able to care for herself. Eight years before, she had gone off to a local fair with her two-year-old son. She came home alone. No one knew if he was kidnapped or just got lost. He was never seen again. After a while Doe remembered the story of the missing child – Doe's aunt ran the safe house – and the pieces of the puzzle started coming together. A birthmark confirmed Bill's identity as the missing child and he was reunited with his birth mother. However, he continued to live with Doe, at his request, because his mother was not able to care for him herself. He had never been to school and, when he moved in with Doe, was desperately sick, in and out of hospital. On several occasions she was told he was dying.

A few months later the Christian Hospital and safe house contacted Doe about another little ten-year-old boy with AIDS. His parents were already dead and he had been so ill in hospital it was assumed he would die too. Unexpectedly he rallied, but had no one to take him in on his discharge from the hospital. So Chan also joined the family home. From February until July 2010 Doe fought tooth and nail with the doctors, who said both children were dying and not worth wasting medication on. They were skin and bone, in and out of hospital, needing intensive love and care. In the end Doe's persistence worked and in August 2010 they started medication. We visited regularly and I could not believe the difference. Within months of treatment I found two lively eleven-year-olds, fit and healthy. By the beginning of the school year in May 2011 they were both well enough to enrol in Year 1; neither had ever been to school before. These two little boys are an amazing testimony to Doe's love and care for these children but also her dogged determination to advocate for them and get the treatment they deserve.

It is not always easy though. In August 2011 Pupa developed pneumonia and died at home. The little family was devastated by losing her. When Ben was eighteen he left school and moved to work in the city. He wanted to live a little! He had missed out on his childhood. But it was hard for Doe to have a teenager who was influenced by his peers and should have been caring for his younger siblings. I look at Tom and the restrictions on his life because of his disability. In the UK he would have every piece of equipment imaginable and would be at a school that could help him reach his potential. In Thailand he has very little. Should we have taken him to a place where he would have get a good education and one day perhaps be able to be more independent? I think not. He has a family who love him and he is content.

In 2012 two more children moved in. Sos was six. His mother died and his father became resistant to treatment. For a while his dad was one of Doe's most committed volunteers, helping others with HIV. When he became too sick to care for Sos, the little boy moved in with Doe. The father is now also dead. About the same time Poe, a five-year-old girl, lost both her parents within two weeks. She had no other family and so she too joined Doe's family. She is the only girl and is doted on by her big brothers!

Doe is an amazing woman and one of my closest friends. When we moved to Sangklaburi I quickly recognised a kindred spirit. She has what I often describe as Christ-like compassion and common sense. She is also a well-trained jungle medic, who is skilled at both diagnosis and treatment; I would rather go to her than many doctors I know. So when I was looking into the situation of doing something at a community level for people living with HIV and AIDS, she was the obvious person to talk to. It became clear very quickly that there were many people living with AIDS who had no support and no understanding of the disease or how to care for themselves. The border areas were about fifteen years behind the rest of Thailand, as far as AIDS education and treatment were concerned, and on the Burmese side there was nothing. Ignorance and prejudice were bad in north-east Thailand but far worse on the Burmese border, where rumour had it that people were killed if they were known to be positive. Add to this the fact that the majority of the population around Sangklaburi are not Thai and have no status or rights, those who were HIV positive were doubly vulnerable. They were afraid to go to the hospital and when they were dying their families did not know how to look after them and were usually terrified of catching this killer disease.

Another characteristic that Doe has is stubbornness and a determined resolve to fight for the best for her patients. She will not allow them to be fobbed off by uncaring medical staff, or refused the treatment they have a right to, as was the case with Bill and Chan, and many, many others. She understands the importance of helping people to die well and in the early days they all died. She walks with people as a counsellor, a medical advisor, a nurse, a teacher and a friend. She prays with them and for them and she is on call twenty-four hours a day, seven days a week. People come because they know they can trust her.

Out of those early visits, the Sangklaburi Community AIDS project was birthed. In 2013 there were one hundred and four infected people being cared for plus their extended families. The project advocates for patients' rights, accesses medication, arranges hospital visits, cares for patients in hospital, provides food and supplies for those too sick to work, teaches nursing care to families, arranges funerals, supports the bereaved and cares for the orphans. Doe has two other staff members, both of whom are HIV positive, as well as ten volunteers. She earns a pittance but does not do it for the money. It is a genuine love for the unlovely and outcast that is her motivation. Funding for all aspects of the project comes through donations from people in Thailand and all over the world.

Of course, when you fight for the rights of those whom society sees as outcasts, you make enemies. The Karen culture, like the Thai, does not see speaking straight as a virtue. As far as the well-being of her patients is concerned, Doe always speaks straight. For many, particularly those in the church who do not have a vision for outreach or for holistic mission, Doe is a troublemaker and they are suspicious of what she does because they do not understand it. That is painful and has caused both of us to shed many tears.

There was, however, one church leader who understood – a close friend of ours called Zaccheus. His church was about six miles away from Sangklaburi. One day he turned up at our house with a young woman on the back of his motorbike and explained that she had recently been diagnosed as HIV positive. Her parents were distraught. They were Buddhist but they brought their daughter to Zaccheus because they said, 'Christians help people,' – and asked him to help. Zaccheus brought her to us, but not to hand her over so we could be the answer to the problem. Instead, he said the church wanted to help but knew nothing about AIDS and were afraid. Could we please teach them how to help? It was a wonderful invitation.

We conducted three seminars in the church on what HIV is, how it is spread, why we do not need to be afraid of people who are infected, and how to help. After the first seminar, church members were already in the young girl's home looking after her child, cooking her meals and cleaning the floor. They cared for her beautifully until the day she died. And ten years on, the church community were still looking after her daughter, with a little support from the AIDS project. That church continued to look after several others in the community who had AIDS and were a wonderful example of Jesus' love and concern for the sick.

Not only was the church influenced by the seminars, but the village head man got to hear about them. He invited us to give public seminars in the local temple. I remember the temple was on the top of a steep hill with no road access. We climbed it, arriving at the top puffing and panting, expecting no one to be there because the place was so pitch dark and silent. The power supply was a car battery and the lights were fairy lights and the odd small bulb so we had to look carefully before we realised it was packed – men, women and children, and all around the edge were the monks in their robes. They listened transfixed as we used stories and visual aids, including a demonstration using Coke bottles, to explain how AIDS is transmitted. We played games and we helped people to understand how to keep safe and why we should not treat people with AIDS badly. On the second occasion we talked about safe sex and using condoms. To this day Rachel will not eat small Thai cucumbers as she says watching our demonstration of condom use, using said cucumbers, traumatised her for life as far as cucumber-eating is concerned! The funniest thing about that particular evening, other than the monks practicing putting on condoms, was the disappointed children, who thought the condoms we handed out at the end were sweeties. Who knows how many lives were saved by those seminars or how many people's attitudes were changed. One thing for certain was that the relationship between the local Christians and the Buddhists was strengthened in the combined effort to fight the spread of this disease and love those suffering from it.

As well as churches and temples Doe and I gave AIDS education seminars together in a variety of other venues. The boarders in the high school hostel in Sangklaburi really got into the activity that involves one person lying on a huge piece of paper and having the outline of their body drawn around them. They fill in the picture of the person – some very imaginatively – and give it a new name; then they write their hopes and dreams for the person. They have to think how an HIV diagnosis might affect those hopes and dreams and, finally, what they could do to help the person with HIV achieve their hopes and dreams. It's a great activity – fun, but also gets them thinking.

Whenever we did AIDS education with teenagers we always offered the opportunity for them to ask questions, emphasising that we were fairly unshockable. I guess in a way that is like a red flag to a bull and so some always tried to shock. One particular young man asked me one such shocker – I am sure just to see what my reaction would be. He asked if it was possible to catch AIDS if one had sex with someone who was HIV positive, after they were dead. Actually it was a good question because it gave me the chance to talk about how long the virus lives for in the body after death – and how long out of the body, etc. Maybe the reason he kept coming back to visit us for years after he left school and we lived in Bangkok was because he realised I was serious about being willing to answer any question as far as I was able. Also I did not give him the satisfaction of looking shocked!

Brothels might be the last place you would think of going to give AIDS education, but actually in a country where the vast majority of HIV infection spread is through the sex trade, they were probably a good place to start. Teaching prostitutes how to take control of their own bodies and use condoms properly may well have saved several of their lives.

Alongside teaching about HIV and AIDS I was also involved in seminars with women, teaching them about sexuality and how their own bodies work. It amazed me how little women know about their own anatomy and physiology. Sex for many Thai women was a trial you put up with as part of the marriage package, and I was amazed when an educated professional – a nurse, in fact – told me she had no idea that women could have orgasms. I do not think my seminars probably covered that in much depth, but I was pretty graphic about a lot of things so I am sure the subject was mentioned. The training was good fun and really liberating for a lot of the women to discover what is where and what it does! We also talked about things like how to check your breasts for lumps, getting regular smears, what is abnormal and should mean a trip to the doctor, and the signs and symptoms of menopause and how to deal with them. Very practical stuff.

One of our most unusual but fun ways of teaching about AIDS was through special events that we organised in both Sivilai and in Sangklaburi. The Christian Communications Institute (CCI) is a department of Payap University in Chiang Mai. They use traditional dance and drama or *likay*[37] to present Bible stories and to explain the gospel. In the early nineties, as we began to see more and more people testing positive for HIV and AIDS, Sivilai church came together with the hospital and public health department to try to do something to address the issue. In the end the church was asked to put together a

---

[37] like a combination of opera and pantomime; very popular throughout Thailand

project because, as the government officials said, 'Christians know how to care for people at a grassroots level.' We decided we needed to raise funds and launch the project at the same time.

Using traditional dance and drama to present Bible stories.

So, I sent a challenge to CCI: 'Please come and perform a Christian likay that also teaches people about AIDS.' They rose to the challenge and travelled all the way from Chiang Mai with their whole troupe. They built a stage on the town sports field and they camped out in the church. On opening night, a famous pop star, who happened to be visiting the local member of parliament, opened the evening's programme – a great way to pull in the crowds. For two or three nights we had an audience of two thousand people sitting on their mats on the field hearing both about Christ and also about HIV. It was amazing. The money we raised formed the initial funding for the home-based care project we started in partnership with the hospital and public health department, which was managed by a committee made up of the local government agencies involved plus the church. The committee oversaw the money so that the church team could use it. The project was still going over twenty years later.

Near to the end of our time in Sangklaburi we invited CCI to come there and teach about AIDS. They spent time in local schools and again performed for a couple of nights on the sports field. The hospital opened up an empty ward for them to sleep in and fed them too. It was once again a wonderful joint venture to put on a great event. The crowds were not so big but still many heard the message.

CHAPTER SIXTEEN

Partnerships in Mission

In many Western countries 'missionary' is considered by some to be a politically incorrect word. There is the feeling that missionaries are from a past era associated with empires and colonialism. Who are we to assume we have something to offer people cross-culturally? Is it arrogance, as some would claim? Others would say that in this world of globalisation and improved communication there is no need to go through the pain or discomfort of crossing cultures. Surely communication of the gospel can be done through technology, in sound bites, via video or Internet, in the same way as other communication happens these days. Why would anyone bother to learn a new language or be immersed in a different culture?

In countries like Thailand, 'missionary' is not considered a politically incorrect word. Many missionaries, both past and present, are highly revered and respected, and on the whole the Thai church is grateful for its missionary heritage. However, that heritage has, in some areas, left images of missionaries that are not always helpful. Sadly, it seems that in many areas of the church in Thailand, missionaries were seen as either superheroes, willing to do and fix anything and everything, or as Santa Claus, willing to provide everything and anything. In our idealism we did not see ourselves as either and certainly did not want to be seen as either. In hindsight we have certainly been guilty of perpetuating the myth and behaving like superheroes or Santa Claus, to some extent. It seems almost unavoidable if you encounter a situation of need and have the money, skills or power to help. Hopefully, over the years we have grown in wisdom as to how to use our money, skills and power so that people do not automatically picture us in skin-tight Lycra suits or in bright red outfits with bushy beards. I think this image will always be there in Thailand as far as missionaries are concerned. Maybe this is partly because within the Thai culture there is a deeply engrained concept of patronage. This means it is culturally expected that someone respected and looked up to, like a teacher or leader, will 'look after' those beneath them in whatever form that 'looking after' takes.

When we were sent to Thailand we went as mission partners, the physical embodiment of a partnership initially between the Church of Scotland, and latterly Interserve, with the CCT. We did not go as pioneers to start our own work, independent of local believers and local leadership. We went to serve the national Thai church and to submit to it, warts and all. It was not always easy by any means. There were many times when we would have loved to have given up and done our own thing. There were many times when we despaired and got frustrated, and other times when we were hurt so much we cried. But fundamentally we passionately believed, and continue to believe, in cross-cultural mission that sees mission partners serving the local church – both small grassroots local churches and the national church.

One vivid picture of partnership and service was Mike's ordination. During our time in Sivilai, the presbytery leadership invited Mike to apply for ordination. After going through all the processes required, including taking exams in Thai and a probation period, he was ordained as a CCT minister in 1997. The service took place in Sivilai church, where Mike was ordained by presbytery leaders in the presence of Dr Sint, the General Secretary of the CCT. Rev. Sandy McDonald, the Moderator of the Church of Scotland, with his wife Helen and Chris Wigglesworth, the General Secretary of the Board of World Mission of the Church of Scotland, were also there, having travelled all the way from Scotland. It was so exciting to have the Scottish church leaders there, but it was the Thai church leaders who laid hands on Mike and ordained him. Many other guests came, including a bus full of members of the International Church of Bangkok (ICB). It was very humbling that so many people were prepared to endure a ten-hour drive each way in order to join us for the service. I will never forget the ICB group singing *I, the Lord of Sea and Sky*. It was the first time I had heard what has become one of my favourite hymns – a personal call to serve wherever God sends. Geoff Bland, a fellow missionary in the presbytery (and the owner of the bath tub I had borrowed a few years before), prayed for Mike, and his prayers touched our hearts. The congregation organised an amazing feast – as usual! – and church members were wonderful hosts. In 1998 Mike was presented with his certificate of ordination at the General Assembly of the CCT. He was honoured to carry the CCT flag in the procession of newly ordained ministers and wore his blue robes with pride. He has always seen the CCT as his church and has sought to serve the Thai church to the best of his ability.

We assumed this was what everyone did, but our year in language school introduced us to many missionaries from all over the world who had come to 'save Thailand' with no reference to the Thai church. Granted the church is very small – less than one per cent of Thai people are Christian – but it exists, is organised and has a vision to reach out. The Thai church needs people who are committed to working with them, not people who look down on them and go off and do their own thing, which is not necessarily the vision of the local church.

About six months after we arrived in Thailand we attended a conference for all the mission partners working under the CCT. Dr Sint, the General Secretary of the CCT at the time, stood up at the first session and said something that really shocked us and everyone else there. Thai people rarely speak straight so what he said was even more surprising. He announced that he would really like to send all mission partners home. After a long, pregnant pause he went on to say that he would then just invite back those who were willing and committed to work under the CCT's vision and not just follow their own agendas. He acknowledged that his idea was not practical or possible but he then talked about how rare it was to find mission partners who took seriously the theory of partnership with the Thai church and actually lived and worked as if they believed it. Many years later he also talked about how frustrating it was to him when people 'played' at being mission partners and did not commit for the long-term. He felt strongly that he did not want people coming to serve for less than four years, because it takes at least two years before language proficiency and understanding of Thai culture are at a level to be remotely useful. Certainly, in this church leader's eyes, language learning and immersion in culture were non-negotiable for cross-cultural mission partners. But there was no question of him not wanting people to come. He just wanted the right people with a true desire to serve. Partnership in mission, involving long term cross-cultural workers, is still something that is valid and has a place.

Contrary to Dr Sint's request for long-term commitment, long-term mission counted in years is, for many agencies, a thing of the past. Now anything over about three months is considered long-term and short one or two-week 'mission trips' are very common. Local-to-local partnerships between churches or institutions in the West and the developing world, getting rid of the need for mission partners at all, are the popular way to go. These local-to-local partnerships can be enriching for everyone involved. However, from our experience, the person who has crossed from one culture to the other and understands both languages and cultures still has an invaluable part to play in being a bridge, bringing people together as he or she interprets the two worlds one to the other, in order to facilitate local-to-local partnership. Without an experienced 'bridge' person there are huge opportunities for things to get lost in translation.

In order to be that bridge we have always felt that our job involved two complimentary and equally important parts – what we did in Thailand and how that impacted the church in Scotland. You see, we did not go overseas because we believe we have all the answers. We went to learn as much as to give, and to bring that which we learnt back to the church in Scotland. We have, since we first left Scotland for Thailand, been in partnership with up to forty local churches, predominantly in Scotland but a couple in England too; churches that have prayed for us and written to us, encouraged us and given financial support to our projects, and even to us when it was needed; churches made up of people whom we count as close friends as they have walked our journey with us; churches who, by being with us in the ministry, can say it is as much their own work as ours. But it is not just what the churches in the West can give to us, to our work and to Thailand. As we have been changed and challenged, moulded and had our world views expanded, so too have, we hope, our partner churches at home.

We have tried to keep in touch with family, friends and churches primarily by writing the *Fish Wrapper* – our regular newsletter. In the early days, when we had more time on our hands, a few select people also received the *Fish in the Wrapper,* where we discussed issues and bared our souls. Since she was about eleven, Rachel has contributed *The Minnows* – her own newsletter to go with the *Fish Wrapper*. We visited churches in Scotland every couple of years and organised well-attended day conferences. We were always aware that we needed to be honest and not just present the rosy picture, but present it as it really was: struggles and difficulties, failures and frustrations, alongside the joys and successes. These partnerships have been invaluable to us and, we hope, to our partners in Scotland and England.

Among the many visitors we have had over the years have been people from our partner churches, some who have come to Thailand on holiday, and others who have come specifically to encourage us. We also welcomed several groups and teams. On one occasion, when we were in Scotland, Mike was invited to attend an elders' conference being run by Barclay Church in Edinburgh, one of our partner churches. It was just after we left Sivilai and they wanted him to talk about and, if possible, explain how and why we saw such incredible church growth. As a result of that conference, Barclay sent a team to Thailand for two weeks with the particular remit of learning how the church was growing in Thailand, in order to apply some of the lessons to church life in Scotland. The team took their remit very seriously. They visited Sivilai and interviewed church members – both new and old. They stayed in people's homes, something that pushed several of them outside their comfort zones. As far as language barriers allowed, they got to know church members and what they felt had been the reasons for church growth. They also visited Sangklaburi where we were living at the time and spent time talking to church leaders and visiting many different congregations. The minister of Barclay was on the team. It was the first time he had ever travelled outside of Europe and the trip was transformational for him and the church.

During one of the Barclay team's visits to a small village church, a Karen woman appeared with a basket of cross-stitch which she hoped to sell to the visitors. Carol, the missionary who lived in our house before us, had taught some of the Karen women to do cross-stitch. However, they had no market. Amazingly it turned out that Helen, the member of the team who noticed the cross-stitch, was herself a cross-stitcher! She was amazed at the quality of the work and got excited about possible market potential in Scotland. And so Kwai River Handicrafts was born. Women sitting in a small bamboo house in a village on the Thai Burma border sew exquisite cross-stitch designs which are then sent to Scotland. In Scotland women volunteer to mount the cross-stitch onto cards, package and price them, and then others sell them. All the profits go back to the Karen sewers. As I write, the project has been going for sixteen years and the cards still sell well. This is a project that really excites me as it is such a great symbol of partnership between two groups of women on opposite sides of the world.

Barclay Church sent a second team several years later when we were living in Bangkok. Their remit on this second visit was to cement a local-to-local partnership with Sathorn church, the church Mike was attending at the time. The elders at Sathorn made the Scots very welcome and a group of Sathorn church members joined the Barclay team as we took them to visit various projects in Bangkok and up on the border in Sangklaburi. For many of the Sathorn church members it was the first time they had visited projects such as Siam Care, who care for people living with AIDS, or CCD, caring for disabled children. Their eyes were opened as much as those of the visitors from Scotland. The same happened when we visited the border – many of them had never seen the poverty or the suffering that they were faced with within the church. It was moving to sit together with the two groups from Bangkok and Edinburgh and talk through each day, looking at God's word and praying for the people and situations we had come across. It helped build a church-to-church partnership in a way that could never have happened by email or letter – and possibly not even by someone visiting, without 'bridge people and bridge shared experiences' to bring them together in understanding and relationship.

Most of the teams that visited us in Thailand were from a particular church. However, we had one team that was made up of people from several different churches. In Sangklaburi we lived on a church compound consisting of about forty acres of land. The government had never issued land ownership title deeds. Soon after we got there they made a ruling that in order to make sure land was not confiscated, it had to be properly fenced and shown to be put to good use. For a piece of land that size it meant over a mile of fencing. It seemed an impossible task both in financial terms as well as time and labour. So we put it to the Church of Scotland. A generous donor agreed to pay for the necessary supplies, and the Church of Scotland Board of World Mission recruited and sent a team of people to help build the fence. Fourteen came from Scotland aged between eighteen and fifty. We added to that a team of about thirty Karen young people and set them to work! It was the hottest time of the year and they worked eight-hour days lifting and carrying seventy-kilogram fence posts. I was constantly cooking for sixty people, three meals a day, for two weeks. The Scots got used to rice for every meal – except for the couple of mornings they introduced the Karen workers to porridge! They did an amazing job and the full mile-and-a-half fence was finished on time. Several of the team have returned to Thailand since the work camp; some more than once. For all of them, and us, it was a life-changing experience.

CHAPTER SEVENTEEN

Our Expat Life in All Its Manifestations

Living in a culture other than one's own is always life-changing. Business people, forces personnel, diplomats, teachers in international schools, students, volunteers, refugees, missionaries; the list goes on. Some do everything they can to immerse themselves in the new culture. Others live entirely in their own cultural bubble, separated in every way possible from the culture of the country where they reside. Many are somewhere in between, dipping their toes in and out of the host culture, enthusiastically learning about history and exploring the city or town where they live, but also at times retreating to the familiar and comfortable. They are enriched even though they are not immersed completely. Some choose to live in a certain way, others seem to have the way they live thrust upon them.

Early on in our time in Bangkok we went to a drinks party hosted by a couple working with a large petroleum company. The wife was a doctor I had worked with in London, but she had given up medicine to follow her husband's job. I asked her how she was getting on with her Thai language study and generally learning about the culture. She explained that the company discouraged people from learning Thai and how it was not worth trying as they knew they would be moved somewhere else in two years. This big multinational did not want people to be get involved locally or to put down roots – they expected one hundred per cent loyalty to the company with no distractions. So their policy was to keep people moving somewhere new before they could develop other loyalties. It was a million miles away from the expectations we had of cross-cultural living.

In our enthusiasm, and probably our arrogance, we were determined that this would not be us! When we moved to Sivilai we were adamant that we wanted to live with the people amongst whom we worked. We wanted to live like them, aspiring to a simple lifestyle; to get alongside them, understand their struggles and joys and be a part of the community. To a large extent we managed. And surprisingly it was not too difficult. We did not feel we made many or difficult sacrifices. We quickly settled into the local ways of shopping (daily in the market), cooking (on a charcoal fire or a single gas ring), washing up (in cold water in a bowl on the ground behind the house), bathing (throwing cold water over ourselves), travelling (on bikes or a motorbike), sleeping (on a mattress under a mosquito net) and managing without mod cons like running water, a flushing sit-down toilet (we squatted!), telephone, television and Internet. We never felt these things were hardships.

A group of young people from the International Church in Bangkok (ICB) once came to stay with us early on and helped to dig our well for us. They thought of it all as an adventure and we had great fun together. But the one thing that horrified these Bangkok expat kids more than anything else was that we could not buy bacon! Maybe that is why I appreciate eating bacon more than most now we live in Scotland.

We realised afterwards that privacy was something we had sacrificed more than anything else, particularly when we were living with church members. It seems to be such a Western concept, and something we tend to expect, or see as a right. Our experience is that you soon get used to not having any privacy and develop strategies for coping. For example, we took long walks in the fields when we needed to have a private conversation or an argument, which would entail raised voices – very un-Thai!

One close friend reflected on the sacrifices we had made when living in Sivilai. We initially disputed having made *any* sacrifices but he said, 'You have sacrificed the company of people of your own culture.' It was true, and we noticed it particularly once we had Rachel. It was not that we were lonely – we had friends in the village – but we had no peers of our own cultures[38] who understood how we wanted to bring Rachel up. We had no one to talk to about the fact that she did not sleep through the night until she was four years old. When we tried the 'sleep plan' there were people banging on our door within ten minutes of her starting to cry! We had no one to ask advice about discipline or diet. We knew there were some aspects of the Thai way of bringing up children that were not for us. For example, Thai toddlers do not sit down to eat; they wander around and whoever is feeding them follows with a bowl of food, spooning mouthfuls in whenever possible. But we had no one to talk to about how *we* should do it. We have a gracious God, who knew what we needed and I suppose provided it in other ways. At the time I do not think we realised how hard it was.

Since moving to Scotland I have, at times, found myself observing groups of young mums chatting and sharing experiences with each other. I have surprised myself by the emotions I have felt; almost a sadness or wistfulness that these relationships were ones I never experienced at that stage of my life. And then I remind myself of God's grace and how He blessed us in so many other ways that I would never want to change.

Living in Sangklaburi was different. The people with whom we worked also became close friends. Our house, although still Thai-style, was more comfortable. We had running water and a hot shower! We had a sitting room with a sofa and chairs and we had a comfortable bed. Despite working just as hard and having just as many different stresses, we did not feel the need to get away in order to survive. We could relax much more easily in our own home than we could in Sivilai. As well as our local friends, there was also an expat community that we got to know; in fact, two expat communities. As already mentioned, there was a missionary community based around the Christian Hospital and the NGO community based around the refugee camps. We got to know people in both. Even that was a cross-cultural experience involving friends from Australia, New Zealand, America, Taiwan, Korea, India, Argentina, as well as England. And it was not always easy. When you are a foreigner living in a small village or town you are an oddity and it is rather like living in a goldfish bowl. Your life is

---

[38] Mike and I are from different cultures.

scrutinised by all. Living with a small group of expats from different places, cultures and backgrounds means inevitably that there are tensions and these are exacerbated because everyone is watching how you relate to these people, with whom you did not necessarily choose to cohabit! Often the stresses and strains between the expats were more painful than any of the stresses of working with the Karen, Mon, Burmese or Thai around us. Despite the difficulties it was also very enriching and we value enormously what we learnt from the people we met and served with.

———————

We were genuinely happy immersed in village life. But despite our best efforts we were always different. Not just with our different-coloured skin and our different mother tongue. *We could leave.* One of the reasons we got a car was so that we could get away. For most people around us, going as far as the nearest town was an adventure. In Sangklaburi those without Thai citizenship were literally forbidden from crossing the district border. There was no concept of holiday or days off. We learnt the hard way, by getting exhausted, that we needed days off. We were different. We could up and go whenever we wanted or needed to. So throughout our time in Thailand we lived a life of confusing contrasts – almost a double life.

Getting away often involved staying in fancier hotels than we would ever have dreamt of in the UK. It was so different from our normal lifestyle. We visited hotels with air conditioning, which we appreciated, not just for the reprieve from the heat, but because air-conditioned rooms are quiet; with swimming pools and Western food; and with TVs! Not only did we stay in nice hotels to get away, but often missions conferences were held in beautiful resorts by the sea or in the mountains – total luxury. In the end the definition of a really posh hotel for our kids was one that had cheese on the breakfast buffet and a chocolate fountain at lunch or dinner; foods that they never got any other time. They were spoilt at the hotels – but the rest of the time they were equally happy to get water from the well and eat sticky rice with their hands, sitting on the floor with everyone else.

The children's 'home away from home' in Bangkok was the Bangkok Christian Guest House; a familiar place with staff they knew and loved and a sense of security and freedom in a big city. It was a great place to meet people and network with other missionaries from around south-east Asia and visitors from churches around the world. We got to know the managers well over the years and on a number of occasions I 'babysat' the guest house whilst the incumbent managers took a break. On one such occasion I managed to lose a guest. She literally disappeared, to the great consternation of her husband and friends. We phoned all the local hospitals, contacted the police and everyone they knew. It was very worrying. Eventually, after what seemed like forever, she called her husband. She had decided to travel home[39] early but had neglected to tell him. When she reached Kanchanaburi she realised how tired she was and checked into a guest house, turned off her phone and went to sleep – and slept for twenty-four hours straight. Only when she woke up and saw all her missed calls did she realise the panic she had caused! Looking after the guest house was not usually so traumatic!

We did not always stay in the guest house. Many friends were very gracious hosts, opening up their homes to us. A number lived in luxurious apartments with stunning views over Bangkok, Western-style kitchens and bathrooms, swimming pools and wonderfully comfortable beds! We appreciated their welcome so much. Staying in Bangkok, when we lived upcountry, was always something of a military-type operation, as we tried to fit everything we needed to do into a few days. There were always lots of errands – usually involving trips to Chinatown and a medical supplies shop or pharmacy.

Chinatown is a maze of small lanes, with hundreds of shops selling everything you can imagine. It is vibrant and colourful, noisy and crowded, and always hot. The Samaki Handicraft project in Sivilai sourced most of its raw materials from Chinatown. We got to know the small streets and lanes well and could still lead you to exactly the right shops for handbag clasps, plastic clips, buttons, foam, zips, beads, stiffening material or straps.

When we lived in Sangklaburi most of my errands were medical in nature. Not only did I occasionally buy supplies for the AIDS project but for about three years Doe and I supplied medicines and equipment

---

[39] interestingly, to Sangklaburi – this was a long time before we lived there

for a small but desperately needed clinic deep in the jungle across the border in Burma. I became good friends with the pharmacist at the shop, which I used regularly. She would prepare for my visits, getting the boxes of antibiotics, diabetes and hypertension drugs, painkillers and other supplies ready for me. She always knew me as 'Jane from the border' and would often throw in extras like thermometers or dressings, as her way of supporting the work.

Other errands involved visits to the Bible Society to get bibles in different tribal languages, meetings at the CCT, renewing our visas and having medical checks. As well as errands, trips to Bangkok also had to include as much fun stuff as possible. The obligatory Burger King or Pizza Hut meal, a trip to the cinema, walks – or, in Mike's case, running – in the park, getting to a church service in English, shopping for life's essentials that we could not get at home – for example, muesli, shower gel, cheese and bacon – and seeing friends all had to be fitted in. We usually returned home exhausted but satisfied we had used the time well. When we eventually moved to Bangkok it took me a couple of weeks to realise I did not have to pack everything into just a few days.

Interserve talks about sending people to the hard places. Certainly they have mission partners living in what I would imagine are the hardest places to live in the world. I had never thought we lived in particularly hard places. And after village life, Bangkok seemed to be a luxurious place to live: Starbucks on every corner, thirty cinema screens within a fifteen-minute walk of our flat, supermarkets that seem to stock everything, albeit at a price; hardly a hardship posting. But once again I think it depends on how you choose to live. For our first five years in Bangkok we lived in a tall, thin townhouse with four flights of stairs. The house itself was roomy but basic. The kitchen was like a small ship's galley, and the air con (in those rooms that had it) was noisy and expensive. We were happy there. We had space to open up our home and have people for meals or to stay. Friends from the villages felt comfortable and at home, and many of them came, whether to visit us or for hospital appointments or church and mission meetings. It was wonderful to be able to offer hospitality. We lived down a narrow lane off a busy road in the business district of the city. We got

183

to know the neighbours and the local shopkeepers and street vendors. It was our community and we felt at home – even happily going to the local street market early in the morning in pyjamas, like everyone else did.

However, it was interesting that when one of our mission leaders visited, he commented that he thought we really were living in a hard place. In some ways, despite our happiness there, he was right. There is an intensity about living in a Thai community in Bangkok: noise that never lets up, smells that pervade the atmosphere, people everywhere. It's a city that never sleeps. Maybe that is why many expats choose to live in tall condominiums and tower blocks, way above the grittiness of daily life. As well as the physical surroundings there is, at times, almost a palpable oppression. It is hard to describe – a spiritual heaviness. Certainly the fears that are deeply ingrained in many Thais must affect their surroundings: fear of the spirits, fear of their own karma, fear of poverty and exploitation. Yes, Thailand is the land of smiles and people do smile and know how to have fun. But often the smiles hide this fear.

If at times I agreed with our colleague that we were living and serving in a 'hard place', there were other times when our lifestyle seemed far from hard, particularly compared to that of some of our friends. Soon after arriving in Bangkok we joined a small group called CWAP – 'Christians Working Amongst the Poor'. We met together every couple of months for a time of chat, prayer, food and fellowship. In some respects, we felt like interlopers in the group. Yes, we had lived and worked amongst the poorest of the poor in Sivilai and Sangklaburi, but in Bangkok most of our work, except perhaps when I was in the prison, was with the middle class. The others in CWAP were living what we considered to be truly incarnational lives, in the slums of Bangkok. Most of them were with groups like Urban Neighbours of Hope (UNOH) or Servants to Asia's Urban Poor. It was a privilege to be a part of what they were doing as we met together. Their lifestyles were light years away from the glossy magazines, maids, chauffeurs, manicures and lunches that is the norm for many expats. Each family lived in one or two-room houses built over the swamps that are under most Bangkok slums. Their daily involvement in the lives of their neighbours was what we had experienced in Sivilai and Sangklaburi – but the events of those lives seemed more dramatic, more critical, more intense: drugs, street fights, evictions, prostitution, trafficking, alcoholism, abuse, desperation and poverty, right there on their doorsteps and often in their homes. But not just these labels – *people*. Needy people, people with hopes and dreams, people to relate to, to love, people to be Jesus to, people to serve as though serving Jesus. Within our CWAP community – a group committed, as Jesus is committed, to the poor, the outcast, the alien and the exploited – we learnt a great deal and I hope also were able to contribute something too.

Living in a community where very few know Jesus can grind you down. Again we did not realise how hard it was until we moved. For our last two years in Thailand, we lived in a small flat in the CCT compound, next to the church headquarters and within the Student Christian Centre. We lived above the canteen and were a part of the Christian community. We ate with the students and we worshipped with them. Mike joined the small church in the compound and became a part of their leadership team. We were welcomed and loved. It was like a breath of fresh air.

In the hot season[40] of 2010 anti-government demonstrators took over the central commercial district of Bangkok, effectively closing it down. After weeks of stand-off with some isolated violent incidents, the army eventually decided to crack down. All hell let loose and a large part of the city became a war zone with fires burning on the streets, large buildings razed to the ground, snipers shooting from rooftops and petrol bombs exploding. Rocket launchers and grenades were used and in many areas it was impossible to move around. We lived on the edge of the 'red zone'. I was in a leadership role for Interserve at the time and some of the volunteers I was responsible for lived in the danger zone. One young couple was housesitting the Christ Church vicarage and the petrol bombs and sniper fire were all around them. So we made the decision to evacuate the team to the beach. On this occasion people in the UK wrote to us to say how happy they were we were out of danger and they hoped we were having a nice holiday! It was no holiday. The Juniper Tree, where we stayed, is a wonderful Christian guest house for mission workers. They looked after us well. The beach is beautiful and

---

[40] April and May

the pool bliss. But we spent the whole week reading reports, listening to news, checking tweets and keeping up with the situation in Bangkok. It was incredibly stressful, but we could do it all in safety. On our return to our smouldering city there was relief, but it was relief mixed with guilt that we had not stuck it out with our neighbours.

It is always tough making decisions about things like evacuation, which illustrate our privilege of choice. It meant we left behind our neighbours and friends who had nowhere to be evacuated to, nor the means to do so. As expats, however much we think we are really part of community, we can always leave; we are different. In fact, we have had to come to the realisation that we will always be expats. We will always be different. We always have choices, outside support and resources and the ability to leave. Even here in Scotland we feel it. We do not quite fit. It will be the same for our children. Hopefully it has made us more aware of, more conscious of, others who do not quite fit; other expats and aliens in our communities whom we can welcome and help to belong.

CHAPTER EIGHTEEN

Following God's Call

Mike and I were called by God to live and work in Thailand. We did not hear an audible voice and nothing particularly dramatic or supernatural happened that led us to believe He was calling us. But both individually and later together we knew Thailand was where He wanted us to serve Him. Throughout our time in Thailand I can say that we were confident in the knowledge that He had called us to be there. When things were difficult, and humanly we were tempted to run away, we were able to stay. This was because we knew that when we were obeying God we were in the best place we could be for ourselves, for others and for Him, even if it was tough. Sometimes emotions take a while to catch up with that knowledge but in the most distressing circumstances we experienced his peace.

Often over the years we looked back on experiences and realised that we were content in what were difficult circumstances because of the gift of God's grace. It is difficult to describe the deep contentment that we had; even when living in an Isaan home with no privacy, or feeling we could not take any more suffering alongside others, or being attacked unfairly by Christians who did not understand us, or coping with church politics or power struggles; even when living in a city of fourteen million people, when we are really country people, or when we or our children were sick, or when we were on the opposite side of the world from family members in both times of difficulty and times of celebration, or when we were robbed and betrayed by people we had trusted. In all of these times alongside inevitable stress, tiredness, anger and frustration, there was a contentment which must have come from God. We stayed in Thailand for so long, not only because we loved it and we could see how we were being used, but more because when life was really tough we still had a sense of contentment that we were in the right place.

And then it changed. God called us to move on, to Scotland. Again, no audible voices or angelic visions to confirm to us this was what He was leading us to do. In fact, making the decision took lengthy and sometimes heated discussions, prayer and even a friend flying out from Scotland for three days to sit and listen to us battling it out in our hearts and minds, trying to decide whether we had got it right or not. But once we had made the decision together, even though we knew leaving was going to be one of the hardest things we would ever do, we had peace about it.

Once again we had to face the consequences of obedience, once again entrusting them into God's hands: leaving people we loved; leaving work that we knew we could have continued to be useful in if we stayed; leaving knowledge of Thai culture and language that would rarely be used in Scotland; leaving a network of contacts and information collected over years that has little relevance outside Thailand; leaving Thai weather and food! In a way, leaving Thailand was like bereavement; leaving all that had meant so much to us for twenty-five years. And yet, in God's grace He prepared us. Over the last six months we were in Thailand we all felt less at home. Less content.

Things happened that caused sadness and stress, and we found them harder to cope with than ever before. We were robbed. Aylie was attacked by a rabid cat and ended up in hospital for a week. A few months later, following a school water sports trip, she contracted leptospirosis and was very ill. We were betrayed by people we trusted. Things that we had accepted as normal or barely noticed started to bug us: the heat, the traffic, the pollution, the noise. Things that we had never accepted as normal, but had fought to change with passion and energy, suddenly left us feeling hopeless and helpless: the injustices, the abuse, the darkness. We suddenly felt very, very tired. We did not leave Thailand because these things happened. We did not run away from a difficult six months. But when these things happened, we no longer felt the deep contentment or commitment that had helped us to hang in there through previous hard times. In some ways it was as if God helped to loosen our ties. He helped to make it easier to leave, not by ordaining the bad things, but by using the way we responded to those bad things to enable us to move forward into something new.

But alongside this loosening of ties there were also great joys. Although our colleagues were sad to see us go, we saw them thriving in their roles and doing their jobs better than we could have done them. We saw new people arriving and had the privilege of helping them to get settled and passing on our stuff to them! And the greatest joy was the response of Mike's church to our leaving.

Ratchatewi Church was a young church, planted in 2011. There were not many members but they had a passion for Jesus and for reaching others with their faith. When we told them that we would be going to Scotland they realised immediately that this was an opportunity for them as a church to be involved in mission. Ratchatewi Church commissioned us to come to Scotland as their missionaries. They laid hands on us as a family in the context of worship, they prayed for us, they gave us money and they sent us. It was both incredibly humbling and an enormous honour. They have continued to pray for us, show love and support and have even sent money to help with ministry in Scotland. Almost the whole church came to the airport to see us off. Once we had checked in they stood in a circle around us, sang and prayed for us again. They walked with us en masse to immigration and sang for the last time: 'God be with you 'til we meet again.'

We *will* meet again, I am sure. We will be back to Thailand to visit. Maybe one day God will lead us back there to work. But for now we have obeyed His call and are in Scotland. We want to be available for Him to use us here and obedient in whatever He calls us to.

Glossary of Thai Terms

ajan	reverend, teacher, professor	p.25
by	let's go	p.137
chang	elephant	p.26
chinchuk	gecko	p.40
dookay	larger lizard	p 40
fymy	fire	p.137
geow	crystal/glass	p.26
gly/gly	near/far	p.22
goy	Isaan dish made from raw meat	p.80
Isaan	North East Thailand	p.12
jy rorn	hot-hearted	p.28
kaen	traditional Isaan bamboo wind instrument	p.66
khru	teacher	p.25
khun	Mr/Mrs/Miss	p.25
kwan	what 'makes up' the soul	p.68
laap	Isaan dish made of minced meat and spices	p.52
likay	traditional theatre	p.165
ma gin khao	come and eat	p79
maa	dog	p.26
mor	doctor	p.25
mor du	witch doctor	p.94
mutmee	a type of woven cloth	p.126
namtan	sugar/brown	p.32
noi	small	p.26
nong	younger brother/sister	p.25
noo	mouse/diminutive instead of 'I'	p.26
P	older brother/sister	p.25
phubakrong	elder	p.25
pii	spirit or ghost	p.98
pit ben kru	mistakes are your teachers	p.22
saa	handmade paper	p.118
samaki	fellowship	p.126
samlor	motorised rickshaw	p.9
soi	lane	p.33
somtam	papaya salad	p.79
takraw	cane ball	p.53
tambon	small town	p.13
uan	fat	p.26
wai	Thai greeting with hands together	p.27
yui	chubby cheeks	p.26

Find Out More

All Nations Christian College (ANCC).
https://www.allnations.ac.uk/

Christ Church Bangkok. English speaking international Anglican church in Bangkok.
http://www.christchurchbangkok.org/home.html

For information about volunteering or supporting the work at **No Boh Academy** through **Christ Church** see:
http://www.christchurchbangkok.org/Karen.html
or email:
karenministry@christchurchbangkok.org

Church of Scotland World Mission Council
http://www.churchofscotland.org.uk/about_us/councils_committees_an d_departments/councils/world_mission_council

Free Burma Rangers (FBR) is a multi-ethnic humanitarian service movement working to bring help, hope and love to people in the conflict areas of Burma, Iraq, and Sudan. Working alongside indigenous pro-democracy groups, FBR trains, supplies and coordinates Ranger teams to help provide emergency medical care, shelter, food, clothing and human rights documentation.
http://www.freeburmarangers.org

International Church of Bangkok (ICB) English speaking international interdenominational church.
http://www.icbangkok.org/

Interserve International, for both short and long term opportunities to serve God in Asia and the Arab world, with sending offices in many countries around the world.
https://www.interserve.org

Kwai River Handicrafts. For information about where to buy the cross-stitch cards or how to get involved in helping to make up or market the cards please contact Helen Miller via:
authorbehindthesmiles@gmail.com

Sangklaburi Community AIDS project. For information about how to support this project contact Jane Fucella on:
authorbehindthesmiles@gmail.com

Siam Care. Siam-Care is committed to children and families affected by HIV and AIDS in Thailand. They help children to access education and support poor families medically, mentally and financially. They also support prisoners with HIV and AIDS. For more information contact them through:
http://www.siamcare.org/

What Shall I Read Next?

Where Love Leads You
Ruth Stranex Deeth
ISBN 978-1-907509-39-1

When an ordinary young woman gives her life into the hands of Jesus, extraordinary things begin to happen. Suddenly she finds herself taken away from her familiar Western culture to serve a nomadic tribe living in the hills and plains of Amudat, completely oblivious of the Kenya/Uganda border. Ruth faces great challenges in adapting to the culture of the people she wants to introduce to Jesus. In trying to provide medical care, she faces the obstacles of superstitious beliefs and tribal politics, and after a government coup in Uganda she is thrown into jail. However, each of Ruth's challenges gives her an opportunity to express the love of Christ to the people around her.

Diamonds in the Darkness
Pat Nickson
ISBN 978-1-907509-14-8

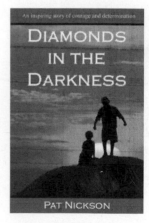

This book tells the story of a remarkable woman who made herself available to God wherever she went. After training as a nurse Revd. Dr. Pat Nickson OBE worked across the world from England to Australia, Bangladesh, Afghanistan and the Democratic Republic of Congo. Congo was her home for more than twenty-five years and the founding of IPASC (the Pan African Institute of Community Health) is her endearing achievement.